Eternal Fruit

Eternal Fruit

SAM AND GINNY CANNATA

XULON PRESS

Xulon Press
2301 Lucien Way #415
Maitland, FL 32751
407.339.4217
www.xulonpress.com

Printed in the United States of America.

ISBN-13: 978-1-6322-1775-2
Ebook: 978-1-6322-1776-9

Contents

Preface

"What did you leave there that was eternal?" How would you answer this question if God asked that of you today? Ginny and I had to face that question from God one day as we were writing the book **Truth On Trial**, which was about our arrest and incarceration in Ethiopia and our subsequent departure with no hope of return.

We were stunned as God turned His searchlight on our hearts and we had to admit that we weren't sure whether we had left anything eternal there or not, despite nine years of intensive missionary work. He pointed out to us that all the sermons I preached, even though they were to thousands of people at my clinics, the witnessing we did and the tracts and New Testaments we gave out freely were only <u>*scattering*</u> seeds. "I want you to plant seeds." He seemed to say to us. Our question to Him was, "Lord, how do we *plant* seeds?"

While we were at home during those months in 1977 writing the book, He led us to three men who helped us understand God's question. One was a man who worked for Billy Hanks, the second was Waylon Moore, the third was Max Barnett, and all these men were advocating and teaching a type of ministry called *discipleship*.

That was over twenty years ago and there weren't many in church and denominational settings who were emphasizing this. Since that time, "discipleship" and now the new term, "mentoring," have become almost by-words in ministry. Despite the new popularity of these words, it seems that most Christians are not willing to embrace the life-style of Jesus and His disciples. And we are convinced that it is a life-style and not a program of filling up notebooks. Jesus' disciples were the ones who started that first century revolution called the New Testament Church.

Little growth results from teaching or even insisting that Christ is also supposed to be Lord of your life. So often we present "The Lordship of Jesus Christ" as an option to discipleship. And it is — alas — far from clear what you would do with lordship if you had it. Obedience and training in obedience form no intelligible doctrinal or practical teaching when people receive Jesus as their Lord and Savior.

A different model was instituted in the Great Commission Jesus left the church. The goal He set forth for the church was to use His all-encompassing power and authority to make disciples. Having made disciples, these alone were to be baptized into the name of the Father, the Son, and the Holy Spirit. With this twofold preparation, they were to be taught to treasure and obey "all things whatsoever I have commanded you." The Christian church of the first century resulted from following this plan for church growth—a result hard to improve upon.

But in place of Christ's plan, historical drift has substituted: 'Make converts (to a particular faith and practice) and baptize them into church membership.' This causes two great omissions from the Great Commission to stand out. Most importantly, we start by omitting the making of disciples, when we should let all else wait for that.

We also omit the step of taking our converts through training that will teach them to do every day what Jesus taught. Now a Christian, that person has become a disciple of Jesus Christ. The disciple is one who, intent upon living a Christ like life, systematically and progressively rearranges his affairs to that end. Discipleship can be made concrete by loving our enemies, blessing those who curse us, walking the second mile with an oppressor—in general living out the gracious inward transformations of faith, hope, and love.

When we went to the mission field in 1958, we were "dedicated" and "committed." We had gone to Bible-believing Baptist churches, colleges, universities and seminary. We had passed the scrutiny of the SBC mission board and were duly appointed missionaries, but somehow, we had missed this discipleship concept.

Our big question now is, "How did we miss it?" Actually, as we look back on our lives, we realize that God was going to have to teach us how to **be** a disciple before we could make disciples. He did this by taking us through some hard times. These would drive us to His throne of grace and would be used to start molding us into the image of His Son Jesus, which we believe He wants to do in everyone's life.

You can read about these things in our first book, **Truth On Trial.** We promised God back then that we would spend the rest of our lives making disciples. But even now, discipleship is not a requirement to be a member of a church or even a missionary representing our churches. It is something you can choose or not choose. You can just live your life without knowing there is so much more excitement in the Christian life when you are investing your life in the life or lives of others. Besides, there is so much more joy when you are being obedient to God's Word.

As you will see in the pages following, it is exciting to find out what God will do through our lives when we are willing to commit our lives to be disciples and then to become disciple makers. This excitement is not just for missionaries and preachers and "full-time" ministers on church staffs. It is for every one of God's children.

Many of us are praying for revival and we believe God wants to send revival in the world today, so why aren't we seeing revival? We are convinced that God is waiting on us to get serious about making Jesus Lord of our lives and then committing our lives to be obedient to His word. This will result in our becoming disciples, as He commanded in the Great Commission. Our first priority will be to make disciples who, in turn will make other disciples **(2 Timothy 2:2)**, which is God's plan for winning the world and would result in a worldwide revival. As we saw God work in miraculous ways among the Murle (a tribe in Southern Sudan), God proved to us that discipleship is His plan both for winning the lost and for bringing revival to unproductive and self-satisfied churches. We don't know how we could have been so spiritually dull to have missed such a vital truth for twenty years of our lives on the mission field. Even if you just read the Bible, it is obvious to you that this is the way Jesus and His disciples lived. This is why their lives caused such a spiritual revolution in the first century.

But we praise the Lord that He did not give up on us, and we even praise Him for the tough lessons He used to teach us, because our own lives have been immeasurably enriched by learning to daily let Him lead in our lives and everyday decisions. When He works through us, we will see things happen we didn't think were possible. Also, we have seen countless other lives blessed as we have shared with them these truths that have been such a blessing to us.

So, the purpose of this book is to show how God can work through His ordinary children to do astounding things in the lives of those around them. Although this book is about us and the Murle, we want to emphasize what our wonderful God can and will do in the lives of people anywhere. Maybe you are like we were. We had been Christians for many years but had not discovered the excitement of being a disciple and making disciples. It is wonderful to know that God doesn't give up on us. He didn't in our case, and He will continue to teach you too if you have missed this truth. We are just ordinary people, but we found that is the kind God can use when we become available.

This book is a remarkable story of what God did in our lives and the lives of the Murle people, who lived in an area around Pibor Post, Sudan. It is truly a story of how **He worked the impossible.** First, it was in our hearts. As missionaries we had spent twenty years with an antiquated and inadequate mission philosophy and approach. And secondly, it was in the hearts of the Murle, who were the most primitive tribal people we had ever worked with in our many years in Africa. And the most remarkable aspect of the story is that He performed these miracles we want to tell you about in less than two-and-a-half years.

Yes, we had been introduced to the concept of discipleship before we went to Sudan, but we were going to a new tribe without any knowledge of their language or culture and I was a medical doctor. In fact, I was the only doctor within 100-200 miles. I knew I would be very busy medically. We didn't know when we started that we had only two-and-a-half years to work at Pibor, but the **Lord knew.**

We were committed to go home with our daughter Cathy when she graduated from high school, to help her get started in a university in the US. We had done this for our two older boys , Mike and Stan. We fully expected to return to Sudan and continue on at Pibor Post after we got her settled. However, shortly after we got home, civil war broke out again in Sudan and spread over the southern part of the country where the Murle were located. Because of that, we never were able to return to Pibor.

Is your life committed to making disciples (or being mentors) as He commanded us in His Word? Perhaps as you read this story, you will be convicted this is what God wants you to do. If you wonder if there is more to Christianity than you have found, we can testify that making disciples is one of the most rewarding and fulfilling things we have ever done. You too can be rewarded in the same way in your life, and we pray that you will. We discovered this is the only way to make "eternal fruit."

Ginny's Note: I wanted you to know before you begin Chapter One that Sam is the narrator of this book. I wrote Chapter 4, the Epilogue, and another small section in Chapter 14 which I marked, but I identify my voice.

Now enjoy!

CHAPTER 1

Journey Into The Unknown

A LONG DAY

I didn't know as that day began that it would become a turning point in Ginny's and my lives. That day, we began an adventure that forever changed us and our concept of what it meant to be missionaries. This journey was to take us to a very isolated area in Africa where God would teach us how to let go of our plans and join Him in **His** work. We didn't know how much He would have to teach us about what it meant to trust Him to be His disciples, and what it would take to make us disciple-makers.

Ginny and Cathy on our adventure to Pibor in a very full car

Maybe it was better that Ginny, Cathy, and I weren't aware of the magnitude of those things when we awakened that morning in Juba, Sudan, to prepare to drive to Pibor Post, a long day's drive to the north and east. We left Juba just after daybreak that morning in March of 1980, but we would not have started so excitedly if we had known the long and tiring trip ahead of us.

We were unable to leave before daybreak because the Sudanese soldiers didn't open the bridge over the Nile River until daylight every day. There was no war going on at that time and as far as we knew, no one wanted to harm the bridge, but this was Sudan. One of their favorite words in Arabic is *Insha'Allah*–"it's God's will" – or "that's the way God wants it," a very fatalistic concept, in my opinion. There didn't have to be a good reason for doing things. They just said, "That's the way it's done."

We knew the first leg of our journey would be from Juba going north, parallel to the Nile River, to Bor, a small town north of Juba. When we left Bor, there were settlements of Dinka villages along the road for several miles, but after a while there were no more people, only dry brush and a very flat plain that seemed to go on forever. To make matters worse, there had been a severe drought in that part of Sudan for almost a year. So, being the dry season, we knew the trip would be a long, hot one.

Yet there was a difference in this trip. We were in unfamiliar country, having only flown to Juba a few days before, and now were going on a road that was completely strange to us. We didn't know exactly where we were going or how long it would take to get there. We had been assured by some fellow missionaries in Juba that the trip could be made in one day, but it would be a long day. Always in the past on our first trips in a new country, we had traveled with someone who knew the way or at least the language, so they could ask directions along the way. Today it was just us with some verbal directions from some missionaries and a few scribbled notes about forks in the road. We had no knowledge of the languages spoken by the people who lived along the road, but our faith was strong and we were on our way.

When afternoon came, it seemed to us like we had been "bundu bashing" forever, because when we left the pavement at the bridge on the east side of the Nile there was no more pavement to be found, just a very long, dusty gravel road.

Bouncing over the "bundu" in a Land Rover in Africa was nothing new to our family. We had been missionaries for nine years (1958-67) in Rhodesia (now Zimbabwe) out in remote bush country in south central Africa. Then another nine years (1968-77) in rural Ethiopia, plus one-and-a-half years in western Kenya. As a doctor during these years, I had learned a lot. Ginny and I had been married twenty-three years by this time, and she had been right alongside me in all of those places. She had birthed Mike, Stan, and Cathy in our mission hospital in Rhodesia, had performed the duties of a nurse in my mobile clinics, had home schooled our children in their early years, was a literacy teacher for rural non-readers, and was a wonderful helpmate. She had done more than her share of driving through the bush in Land Rovers on many occasions.

Cathy, our sixteen-year-old daughter, was a junior in high school. She had mainly grown up in Ethiopia where she had attended boarding school (after her first three years of home schooling) until we missionaries were all forced out of Ethiopia in 1977 by the Ethiopian Communist regime. Being "forced out of Ethiopia" actually means we left after our arrest. You can read about that in our book, **Truth On Trial**. Cathy was used to rough and hard travel through the African countryside, too.

The rainy season in Sudan begins in May and for the two or three months before that, it is unbearably hot, dry, and dusty. When we left Juba early in the morning that day, the temperature was bearable, but by midmorning it was getting very hot. By afternoon we imagined it was something like being in the middle of the Sahara Desert. Our Land Rover was packed solid with food, water, extra diesel fuel, our suitcases and Sugar, our boxer dog. Some of our clothes were on top of all that stuff in a garment bag.

As we followed some of those scribbled directions, we found what we thought was one of those forks the people in Juba had told us about, and turned onto it. The road down that fork was more like a path or a trail than a road, but we were headed east toward Pibor Post. Even the name sounded remote. The British had named it, and during WWII they had a small force there to keep their eyes on the Ethiopian border about sixty miles to the east. Sudan was at that time a British Protectorate and the Italians had invaded Ethiopia in 1936, early in WWII.

We knew Pibor was remote, but we couldn't at that point even imagine how remote it was. We should have had a clue because there was obviously no traffic going toward Pibor or coming from there.

At one point about mid-afternoon, with all the bouncing, one of the Jerri-cans of diesel fuel got dislodged, so we had to stop to straighten out the back end of the car. I had to put the garment bag with some of our clothes up on the roof rack, but I forgot to put it back inside the car when we started again. (I've always had a problem with small details like that.) Needless to say, we never saw those clothes again.

ARE YOU SURE, LORD?

There had been a severe drought in that part of Sudan for almost a year. The dry season was normally somewhat dry, but this year it was twice as dry as normal and we were sure it was twice as hot, too. As we went through this hot and arid countryside, our hearts longed for the cool of the Ethiopian highlands where we had been for nine years during most of Cathy's growing up years. Or the green of western Kenya on the shore of Lake Victoria, where we had spent our last eighteen months in Africa before coming to Sudan. Every day we could look out over miles and miles of water in one direction and green sugar cane fields for miles in the other direction. Those places seemed very far away as we traveled along in this flat country.

Everything was hot and dry, no green anywhere. Farther along, our hearts ached as we passed dead cattle in different stages of decomposition all along the way. By this time, we weren't even sure we were on the right path to Pibor Post. In our depressed and discouraged hearts, another question kept surfacing: "Are we sure that God really wants us in Pibor Post, Sudan?" Maybe we were enduring this terrible, never ending and seemingly worsening journey by mistake. We didn't know anything about Pibor Post except what we had heard from a Wycliffe missionary named Jon Arensen. About eighteen months before, at a guest house where we were staying, he had shown us a few slides of Pibor where he was living. As we had listened to his story about work among the Murle, a semi-nomadic tribe in Southeastern Sudan, Ginny felt maybe God would have us go there.

She felt almost immediately that we should knock on that possible door of service. I had some questions in my heart early on because the term "nomadic" stuck in my mind. God had called us to make disciples, and in all the disciple-ship materials we had been given, none seemed suited to discipling nomads. However, as I prayed about it, God gave me peace about at least knocking on the door. There were several ways God could close that door, and since both of us had said several times, "We will never go to Sudan," I had hopes that He would close the door in one way or another.

However, later Ron and Judy Bodenhamer, fellow missionaries in Kenya, actually were so interested in Sudan they flew to Pibor just to see the place. They confirmed that they too felt God might be calling them there. They believed it was a place of great need and also great opportunities of service. I was willing to go, if God opened the door, but I was still counting on Him to close it for us.

FIRST DOOR GOD COULD CLOSE

In the one-and-a-half years we were in Kenya, I had suffered a ruptured cervical disc after the first six months and a Scottish orthopedic surgeon who had examined me in Nairobi had advised me to return to the US for surgery by. However, in our Preface we shared with you about how God had put into our hands lots of materials about discipleship and into our hearts a whole new concept of ministry. So, making it a matter of prayer, we decided not to go home for surgery unless the pain became unbearable. We wanted to apply these new principles of discipleship and live out this new lifestyle God was revealing to us.

Driving seemed to be the greatest aggravating factor for my back problems, and every week I drove to four rural clinics around Kisumu in western Kenya. So, I canceled my clinics for a month and made reservations at our Brackenhurst Baptist Assembly, about thirty miles from Nairobi, to see if a month of rest would help my disc problem. Also, while resting, I joined the students in the language school and studied the Kiswahili language. When the month was over, we returned to Kisumu and Ginny began doing all of the driving.

(I must tell you: before we headed back to Kisumu, I took the closing Kiswahili language exam and passed it. The students, who had been in class much longer than I had, were not happy about me passing their exam. Oh well. I had discovered that languages came easy for me.)

At the onset of the disc injury, I had experienced very severe pain in my right neck and shoulder and had numbness and weakness in my right arm. But with Ginny driving, instead of getting worse, the pain gradually got better and

I was able to continue my clinic ministry. But changes were coming.

While at Brackenhurst, Ginny and I prayed, asking the Lord to show us His way of ministering through the clinics in the year that remained of our time in Kenya. He led us to drastically change our clinic schedules. We notified each medical officer that after each clinic we would spend the night at their location. I would teach a Bible class to any of the church members who wanted to come to church on the clinic days, after we had seen all the patients. Each of the four clinics had been placed by a church. After the Bible studies, we spent the evenings having fellowship, prayer and family devotionals with the clinic officers and their families. We took food with us, but they always wanted us to eat with them.

Clinic officers were well-trained people who could diagnose and treat most common diseases, and operated the clinic on a daily basis. They would save the hard cases for me since they knew I would be there on the scheduled clinic day. We have learned since, from some of their grown children, having devotionals with the families was some of the most productive discipling we did at that time. Spending time with them was also a very important part of discipleship. During those days, we learned for the first time how to invest our lives in the lives of others over a prolonged period. We realized that, in general, our teaching and preaching in the past had only been "scattering seeds," as God had previously pointed out to us.

When that year was over, since we were due a furlough, we returned to the US for my cervical disc surgery. Also, the decision about being transferred to Sudan deeply concerned us and we were praying earnestly about it. The prospect of cervical disc surgery with all the months of recuperation hovered over us like a cloud.

Before leaving Kenya, I had arranged for a hospital bed and an appointment with a neurosurgeon to be waiting for me in Waco, Texas, where we were to furlough. So, on our first day home, after my appointment with the neurosurgeon, he admitted me to the hospital where they made x-rays of my neck. The next day when the neurosurgeon came to visit me, he asked me some questions and chatted a while. After hearing my symptoms and checking my right arm, he confirmed I indeed had a ruptured cervical disc and under most circumstances would need surgery.

Then he said, "Now, you are a doctor and I am a doctor and I will do whatever you want done. But have you seen your x-rays?"

I assured him that, as I understand it, in most hospitals the x-rays were not shown to the patients even if they had an "M.D." after their name, and this one seemed to have that policy also.

"Oh yes, of course. Well, let's get them in here." He brought the x-rays in and showed me an unusual phenomenon that was taking place between my C5 and C6 vertebrae.

In the year we had waited to learn and practice discipleship principles and lifestyle, a deposit of tough callus tissue had grown between the vertebrae on either side of the ruptured disc.

Then he said, "Now, I will do whatever you want, but in a few months, you will have a better fusion between those vertebrae, without any scar tissue, than I would give you if I operated. So, what do you want to do?"

I said, "I know of about fifty or sixty people praying about my disc problem right now, so I believe this is the answer to their prayers. So, I will just check out of this hospital as soon as you discharge me!"

He promptly did just that. When I called Ginny to come pick me up, she could hardly believe her ears, because she thought I would be there from one to two weeks while I recuperated from surgery. (This was before microsurgery.) We could only praise God for this wonderful miracle from Him. And in fact, since that time I have had no serious problems from the disc.

On the other hand, God had just removed one of the main obstacles that might hinder our going to Sudan. Some may ask, "Why were you so definite about saying you didn't want to go to Sudan?" It was for this reason: we could remember those times early in our mission career when our plane, going to southern Africa, would refuel in Khartoum, Sudan, between midnight and 2:00 AM. When they opened the plane door, at that hour of the morning a hot, suffocating wind would blow into the plane. We had said each time, "We never want to be missionaries in Sudan." Also, Sudan had a terrible track record concerning instability and civil wars, so we let God know way back then that we did **not** ever want to ever go to Sudan. We learned through this experience that you really can't and don't tell God what you want to do.

DOOR NUMBER TWO

Of course, there were other doors God could close. This would be door number two. There was no mission work in Sudan under our mission board, and the whole board had to approve opening up work in a new country. Would you believe? The next month, the mission board approved starting work in Sudan. The second door that could have closed was now open.

DOOR NUMBER THREE

But I was a doctor, and the medical committee of the mission board had just voted not to open any more medical work until all vacancies in the medical field were filled. This was because of a shortage of doctors in most of our established mission hospitals and other medical ministries around the world. There was a good chance the medical committee would refuse to let me start medical work in a new country where a doctor would be one of the first missionaries.

Again, only the Lord could have engineered this one. The next month, the medical committee approved opening new medical work in Sudan. As I reviewed all of this in my mind, I knew without a doubt we were destined to be going to *Pibor Post, Sudan.*

CAN WE FIT IN?

Other concerns kept coming to our minds as we traveled on that hot, dusty road toward Pibor, such as: "What's it going to be like when we get there?" True, we had been missionaries over twenty years by that time, but we had always served under one mission board, and our Southern Baptist board didn't have any work in Sudan. So, this time we had to be seconded to another mission group called ACROSS (An acrostic for **A**frica **C**ommittee for the **R**econstruction **O**f **S**outhern **S**udan) to open this new work. It was an umbrella organization for many different groups serving in Southern

Sudan. We could only get visas and work permits into Southern Sudan at that time through this agency.

Also, we knew there were two families at Pibor. One family was from SIL (Summer Institute of Linguistics – Wycliffe Bible translators): Jon and Barbara Arensen and their three children. They were not under the ACROSS umbrella. The other family was from the Presbyterian mission: John and Gwen Haspels and their three children. We asked ourselves: Can this work? Wycliffe, Presbyterian, and Southern Baptists on the same team? Not only that, it had been hinted by the ACROSS officials that the two families going out under ACROSS would have to live together in the house they owned at Pibor. However, they emphasized that the house was very adequate.

We had seen a picture of Jon and Barbara's house, but we had no idea what the other house even looked like. In our twenty years in Africa, we had lived under many kinds of conditions: cooked on a wood stove in Rhodesia, camped out in the bush in tents many times, lived in government housing in Rhodesia, slept in many rural Ethiopian houses, and had even listened to the termites chewing on the wood in the walls of one of our houses. Yet we had never had the experience of living together with another family in the same house.

The Haspels were there first. Would they welcome total strangers? How would things work out with us and a family with three younger children? What kind of mission house would be adequate for two families? We had stayed in the ACROSS Guest House in Juba during our first days in Sudan. If that was any indicator, we had a feeling this house would be very spartan, to say the least. At this point, if there was a place to lay down tonight at the end of our hot and tiring trip, we would only praise the Lord. Whatever decisions still needed to be made could be tackled tomorrow.

"PLAIN" LONELY

As we traveled along, we kept hoping to meet someone walking along the way, but knew even if we did, communication would be impossible. We didn't know any Dinka (the tribe and language of the people near Bor) or Murle (the tribe near Pibor), nor even any Juba Arabic, a trade language, which most Southern Sudanese would possibly understand enough to give directions. From our time in Ethiopia, we did know Amharic, a Semitic language kin to Arabic, but with very few common words. Fortunately, there were a few, which helped considerably later on that night. Still, just to see someone on this lonely plain would have been encouraging. If for no other reason than to know that other people actually did use this trail.

We knew Pibor Post was east of Bor, but when traveling over a wide plain with no definite road to guide you, you could easily miss a place by twenty to thirty miles. We were getting very tired. We had made a lunch but had eaten it long before. We had some snack food along, plus water, but we weren't looking forward to spending the night in the Land Rover.

Not that we hadn't done that before. We had, but the last time was in Ethiopia. Cathy was a little girl and our son Stan, who was three years older than her, was with us. We had arrived at a muddy area on a dangerous mountain road at night where we couldn't go forward or backward because we were stuck in the mud. So, we spent the night at about 12,000 feet altitude, with freezing winds blowing around and through the poorly sealed Land Rover. We put Cathy and Stan in sleeping bags, but Ginny and I almost froze before morning.

The next morning a government vehicle from Menz (the area where we lived) came along and pulled us out of the mud. They had a gun with them and killed a rabbit out there by the road. They wanted to share a part of the rabbit's liver with us (uncooked) but we gracefully declined the offer. They said it was the best part of an animal. Well, sorry, we didn't agree with that.

Back to the Pibor story: This time, we knew sleeping in the car would be different, but in the opposite way. We couldn't leave the windows open due to thousands of insects, mostly malaria-bearing mosquitoes. We felt we would suffocate with three people and our dog Sugar in a packed car.

UNEXPECTED ASSURANCE ENROUTE

With the sun gradually going down, we just kept going across country, knowing we were going east because the sun was setting behind us. Suddenly we saw some dust out across the plain in front of us. We felt like shouting "Hurray," because it was a Sudanese government vehicle headed for Bor. It was full of police. They stopped and confirmed we were headed toward Pibor, where they had just been. We were glad one of them knew a little English, and also glad to have some tracks to follow, which were faintly visible as we started again toward Pibor. We figure they found our garment bag of clothes, which we never saw again.

Being near the equator there is little or no twilight, so it got dark very quickly. Before long, we couldn't see the tracks, so all we knew to do was to keep going in the same direction. When some stars came out, we picked out the ones we thought were toward the east and kept plodding on in the dark. I'm sure it was imagination, but even the car lights seemed dim.

I was careful, because in the past, in Rhodesia and later in Ethiopia, in the dark, I had dropped our Land Rover in some impossible holes that required another vehicle to pull us out even though we had four-wheel drive. I could see us stuck out here on this plain, not even knowing which direction to walk for help. At Pibor there were two missionary families with vehicles and I knew they would help us, if they could find us. For all I knew, they could be ten miles in any direction. And honestly, I didn't feel like walking even one mile.

A FRIGHT IN THE DARK

Across the wide plain we had seen no trees for hours, only scrub brush like one sees in the western US. But as we drove on, we noticed the stars were being obscured along the horizon. Then our headlights showed some tree trunks. We didn't know where we were but knew there must be a river somewhere near because of the trees. Our lights indicated we were again on a better developed trail among the trees. We knew that Pibor Post was on a river, so this was good news.

All of a sudden, we were confronted by a soldier, who leaped out in front of us with his gun pointed shouting "Kusum!" Fortunately, Arabic and Amharic both use the same term for "halt!" Ginny and Cathy screamed, and I quickly stopped and turned on the inside car lights to show we were not armed. The soldier knew no English, but finally agreed to lead us on to his commanding officer. Fortunately, the officer knew some English and also had been advised of our arrival by the Haspels. He agreed to send a soldier to walk ahead of our Land Rover across the dry river bed the next one-and-a-half miles to the first mission house. There wasn't even a square inch of space for him to sit inside our car, so he had to walk.

THE END OF THE JOURNEY

The lights in that house were a very welcome sight after our seemingly never ending and harrowing trip. The John Haspel Family – John, Gwen, Desta, Chuck, and John John – came out to meet us. It was wonderful to find someone we could speak to in English. They were the American Presbyterian family who lived in one end of the house where we were also to live. They had been notified by radio that morning that we were coming, and they welcomed us. They too had been concerned about us trying to travel by ourselves all the way from Juba to Pibor in one day, knowing we could have easily lost the trail in the dark. They rejoiced with us that the Lord had miraculously kept us on the right path.

It was good to get out of the Land Rover. They invited us in and told us to sit at their long dining table. Even though it was late, they fed us some supper and cold water from their kerosene fridge. It was all very welcome. Our water had become hot even in our thermos. We could hardly believe the journey was over, that we had actually arrived at Pibor Post, Sudan, we were with friends and had a roof over our heads. We prayed together and then fell into the beds they had prepared for us. We knew we had many things to learn about Pibor Post, but that could wait till morning.

CHAPTER 2

Settling In

THE HOUSE – ADEQUATE, BUT SOME BAD NEWS

John and Gwen had walked us around the house before we went to bed, but we were too tired to take it all in. The next morning as Ginny looked around and remembered the hard trip of the day before, she made the comment that perhaps we **were** 100 miles beyond the Great Commission. But we were ready to see where we would spend the next few years of our lives.

The house actually was very big and was shaped like an "E". Now you know that an "E" has five separate sections if you divide the long side of the "E" into two sections. The Haspels had made the middle prong of the "E" their kitchen and dining room and that was where we visited the first night around their table. We were to live in the remaining two sections and actually that would be very adequate, because Cathy would be at boarding school most of the time and would be leaving after a month. Each section was about twenty-five feet long and fifteen feet wide.

As we continued the tour that morning, they shared some bad news about the house. They had killed more than forty scorpions in our part of the house as they prepared for our arrival. And these scorpions were not the small kind either. American scorpions looked like midgets besides this Sudanese variety. What a happy thought! We were soon to learn more about these scorpions, though, when I put my hand on the wall one morning just to steady myself, not seeing the scorpion sitting there. I jerked my hand away immediately, but the sting caused a lot of pain in my hand for about four to six hours. It was better by clinic time that day, so I was able to see the patients in the afternoon.

We all learned to shake out our shoes every morning, in case they had a scorpion in them. But John was in a hurry one morning and laced up his hiking boots before realizing there was a scorpion in one of them. He didn't feel the sting until he had walked toward the back door. Of course, it was impossible to get his boot off quickly, so his foot got all the poison from that large scorpion. Immediately, we took all of the ice we had in our fridges so he could put his foot in ice water. We had been told this was the best remedy for a scorpion sting, so we tested out the theory. He had terrible pain in his foot for almost two days. Of course, I gave him medicine for the pain, but it didn't do much to help him. Those scorpion bites were powerful.

We think the Haspels had as much concern about two families living under the same roof as we did. ACROSS had another house over in town about one-and-a-half miles away and gave us the option of living there. However, in the next few days, after we got a picture of the lay of the land around us, we discovered an old hospital building about fifty yards from the "E" house. It became obvious the doctor needed to live near that building. I didn't plan to make it a hospital, but it would be very adequate for an outpatient clinic with some rooms for patients in case they needed treatment for more than a day. So, we chose to stay in the big "E" house with the Haspels. In the days ahead, when the patients began to come in greater numbers, we knew we had made the right choice.

SOME SHOCKING REALITIES

All cultures are different, but we found out in the next day or two that the Murle culture had more than its share of differences. We had seen Jon Arensen's slides, but realized he had edited which slides he showed us of the Murle work. We knew the Murle wore very few clothes, but didn't get the idea that most of the men didn't wear *any* clothes. Our first few hours and days at Pibor quickly brought home this truth. When the Murle men wanted to really dress up, they put some beads or ivory bracelets on their arms. We were told the British had made a law that the men had to wear a shirt when they crossed the river into town. We never checked that out, but think it was true.

The women did a little better, with a leather loincloth in front and back that went from below their waist down to their upper thighs. Occasionally a few would wear a cloth over one shoulder, but mostly they only had their loincloths and nothing else. However, when they sat, they were very discreet and always brought the posterior loin cloth to the front and covered themselves modestly.

We also found out they had no manufactured possessions except maybe a steel pot for cooking. In the old days they had used clay pots to cook in, but had found that it was better to buy a metal pot than to continually make new clay pots that broke so easily. They used freshwater clam shells out of the rivers for spoons and large gourds for carrying their water. Most families could roll up all of their possessions in a kob skin and carry it on their heads. The kob was an antelope about the size of an American deer that migrated yearly in a fifty to seventy-five-mile circle through the Murle territory. So, the tribe and the kob migration crossed paths two or three times a year.

At this point, we should describe the relationship of the Murle tribe and the kob migration, since it was almost vital for the tribe's survival. At the time we were there, the Murle had no guns and did all their hunting of the kob with spears. There were millions of kob and the Murle tribe and the kob migration worked synergistically. The Murle kept the kob from overpopulating by killing what they could with their spears for food, but without guns they could never kill enough to endanger the species. The kob had become the main source of meat for the Murle and allowed them to develop larger herds of cattle because they didn't need to kill the cattle for meat. Their source and measurement of wealth was their cattle.

We found out later during the rainy season, when the rivers were full, the migration brought many of the kob in our direction and they crossed the river right in front of our house. Since it was easier to kill the kob while they were swimming in the river, there were Murle out on the river-bank every night for two or three weeks, right in front of our house. Many of the animals chose to cross the river at night, so the Murle men were sitting there waiting to hear them splash as they crossed the river. Our son Mike, who had come to Pibor for his summer break from college, even killed one with a borrowed spear.

There was always much excitement during that time of year and also much feasting. Actually, the last two months of the dry season were very lean for the whole tribe because their meager harvested crops had been eaten after a few months. Their faces would be drawn and their bodies very thin until the kob came through. Then it was immediately very noticeable that their faces and bodies filled out quickly.

We decided that in general they were not a very polite people. Their language didn't have very good words for "please" and "thank you." But of course, they had ways of expressing these to each other. So, until we got better acquainted with the language and some of their non-verbal communication, it seemed we were among a very demanding and rude people. Our greatest question to the Lord in those first days at Pibor was, "How are we ever going to make disciples under such impossible circumstances?"

THE BIG "E" HOUSE

I had expressed earlier that we suspected the house would be spartan, but even that might be an understatement. The Haspels told us we were living on an old Presbyterian mission station, which had consisted of the hospital building and three other houses. These were all on the banks of the Pibor River. The hospital was the first in line, then the big "E" house we lived in. The next was a small cement block house that was to be made available later for our friends the Bodenhamers. The last in the line was the Arensens' house, which was smaller but similarly screened in like ours. They had been the first to come to Pibor, about four years before we arrived, to learn and analyze the Murle language in preparation for starting the translation of the Murle New Testament.

The houses were well built and the big "E" was the largest. The walls were built out of stones about eighteen inches thick. The long back side of the "E" was the front of the house and faced the river, about fifty yards away.

The front of our "Big E" house The last missionaries who lived there had left just after the first civil war in Sudan started in the 1950s. In the twenty-five years since then, the thatched roof on the big house had fallen in when the wooden trusses rotted. The window and door frames had also rotted away. So, before we arrived, ACROSS had sent a builder to Pibor with lots of angle iron for steel trusses, wood for window and door frames, lots of mosquito screening, and corrugated iron for roofing and new doors. He didn't replace any of the large window spaces with glass but had put screens in all those big gaps.

So, if you can get the picture, one of our sections of the "E" that faced the front of the house (the long or back side of the "E") was merely a screened-in porch on both sides. The house did have stone walls up to the heights of a lower windowsill

– about three feet above the floor. You can imagine what it was like when the rainy season came and the wind blew. It was difficult to stay dry – until we had a good idea. We lost no time in sharing this idea with Juba.

The next day, we called the ACROSS office on our radio and asked someone there to buy us enough mats to cover the places where the windows used to be. We knew Juba had a market where these mats were sold. The people made them out of reeds. When they arrived by plane, we attached them to the outside of the screens and worked a small rope inside that could be used to roll them up or down from the inside. Cozy. When a blowing rain came, they kept out most of it. At night it was dark in the room until we lit our kerosene lamp. Later we got a solar panel to charge batteries and then we had some small 12-volt fluorescent lights for nights and dark days.

ACROSS had done a good job preparing for the dry season by putting two very large galvanized metal water tanks (about 500 gallons each) on each end of the house.

Our two large water tanks to last us through the dry season They
also installed gutters so the rainwater would drain from the roof into
the tanks. They were going to help very much when the rains finally
started, but were very empty when we got to Pibor. These tanks of
water would be our only source of water besides the government well
in town, where the townspeople got their water, and where we got our
water too, until the rains started and filled our tanks.

In fact, everywhere was very dry. In the river in front of
our house there was one last tiny pool left, mostly lots of
mud surrounding a small amount of thick, muddy water. A
few rather large fish were still alive, just flopping in the mud.
When the Murle didn't even bother with them, we could
imagine they were definitely inedible. There were carcasses
of dead cattle lying around and one of them was just across
the river from our house. The smell was awful when the
wind blew in our direction. We figured the poor cow had
probably died trying to get its last drink of water.

The government well in town, about one-and-a-half
miles away, had a diesel engine that pumped very nice,
clean water with one of the old "donkey" pumps, the kind

used frequently years before for pumping oil in the US. This pump worked as long as there was diesel fuel or no equipment breakdowns, but from time to time it would be shut down for a day or two, waiting for fuel or replacement parts. A couple of times we helped to repair the pump or the engine. From morning to night there were people with water jars in a long line, waiting their turn. There was no way that pump could pump water for the people plus all those dying animals. So, we rationed water at our house. Fortunately, the rains did start a few weeks after we arrived and began to fill our big tanks. We were grateful not to have to go to town anymore to haul water.

We grew to love the Haspel family. Desta was born in Ethiopia and her name means "joy" in the Amharic language. She was ten years old at the time. Chuck was named after his grandfather and was eight years old when we arrived, and John-John was the youngest and only four. Gwen was a nurse, which was very nice, always ready to help me in the clinic when I needed help. However, she was very busy with home schooling Desta and Chuck and caring for little John-John. John was an evangelist and church planter, so they, along with us, had many concerns for the spiritual needs of the Murle.

Because none of us knew how to reach the Murle with the gospel, we began praying together after they put their children to bed. We prayed for the Murle and the overwhelming needs we saw around us. Our knowledge of the language was very poor, so at first everything was quite frustrating. However, when the people heard a doctor had come, many patients began to arrive. Most of the first patients were sick babies. (But I am getting ahead of our story.)

THE TRUCKS ARRIVE

Our belongings were coming on trucks scheduled to arrive later in the month. Fortunately, they arrived before any big rains. However, we did have a scare when it rained small showers two times in the two days before the trucks came. We remembered the wide, flat plain between Bor and Pibor and realized that with some good, hard rains the plain would be nothing but mud and might even have standing water. We prayed a lot about the arrival of the trucks and were overjoyed and so thankful when we heard the engines of the big trucks making their way across the dry riverbed to our house.

So now living would be so much easier with a kerosene refrigerator and freezer, plus a propane stove for the kitchen. Most Americans have forgotten that there ever was such a thing as an "Electrolux" refrigerator, which got cold because of a fire underneath it. Well, in many places in Africa they were still in use and very welcomed and useful. We had to learn how to use them and had to watch them carefully. When they started smoking and fuming (which they always did at some point), we pulled out the tank that held the kerosene and cleaned the wick. As soon as possible, though, we converted our fridge and deep freeze to propane. We did this by putting a Bunsen burner under the cooling units. We were learning all kinds of new angles about bush living.

OUR FURNITURE

For our living room furniture, we had a couple of chaise lounges (the aluminum tubular folding kind that people in the US used on their patios) with a couple of wooden chairs that ACROSS had furnished. We ate meals on a card table and sat on some folding chairs we had owned in Kenya and had sent with our things on the truck. We slept on a foam mattress on a homemade bed (the frame was made from the wooden crate that came on the truck) and had a single bed for Cathy to sleep on. That was our furniture.

When the rains came and the mosquitoes got bad, we had to put blankets on the chaise lounges (we certainly didn't need them for warmth) because the mosquitoes bit us so badly through the straps on the lounges when we sat down. We didn't dare sleep without mosquito nets either. They were truly life savers because malaria was rampant at Pibor. Besides, scorpions might be running around at night, too.

Because it was so hot most of the time at Pibor, we thought a waterbed would keep us cool. After a few months, we had someone buy us one in Kenya, which was flown in to Pibor. We felt with all the hot weather at Pibor we could do without the waterbed heater, but we were wrong. We knew all the people in the US with waterbeds had an electric thermostat to keep them the right temperature. We thought in hot Pibor we wouldn't need such a thing, but found out quickly that sleeping on water just a few degrees below body temperature is too cold. We were sorry we didn't know that. We lived and learned. So, we ended up putting blankets under our sheets on the waterbed to make it possible to sleep on the unheated water. We used blankets in all the wrong places for all the wrong reasons.

A PRIVY PANTRY

Our bedroom was the corner room of our two sections, which formed a big "L." On entering the last section, there was a handwashing sink, and next to that space was a shower. The water for the shower came from a fifty-five-gallon drum rigged up under the eaves of the roof so the rainwater could keep it full. We finally painted it black because the water was still too cold for our American tastes. We hoped the afternoon sun would make it warm enough to be comfortable for our showers. However, it didn't work, because in the rainy season the sun was hidden most of the day.

Sam hung a barrel for shower water, threw a black inner tube on the roof, and connected it to have hot water.

The last little room in that section (you would never guess) was an "inside" deep pit privy! When we first looked at it, we were horrified and decided it must be filled in because we just knew it would smell awful. We figured we could dig a privy outside, like the Haspels had on their end of the house. However, that was not top priority and would have to be done later after more important things were accomplished, like making a frame for our bed and hanging our mosquito nets. So, for the first week we used the indoor privy and were amazed at its design and engineering – there was no smell. Besides that, since it was in our part of the house, it was very convenient, especially knowing that at night there would be scorpions and snakes outside, which was not a pleasant thought. It is amazing what you can get used to. Besides that, there was lots of space around the privy, so we put shelves from floor to ceiling and made it our pantry. Great idea. We could plan meals while in the privy. Do you think that helped us have a much more balanced diet? Actually, it didn't.

WORLDL'S SHORTEST LANGUAGE SCHOOL

We knew there was no way we could make disciples with the Murle without developing relationships, and there was no way to develop relationships without learning their language. When we arrived, the Arensen family – Jon, Barbara, and their three children – were in Juba, and they had only six weeks at Pibor before leaving for their year of home leave. Jon had promised to teach us all the Murle we could learn during those six weeks. We figured that probably wouldn't be very much, since all the language schools we had attended in other countries were at least nine to twelve months. However, the Haspels and we both had learned other African languages, which always helps. We had never heard of a six-week language school and none of us were linguistic geniuses. What to do? No choice but to give it a try.

We were convinced the Lord had called us to Pibor and had given us an assignment to make disciples, as impossible as that now seemed. We had frequently claimed two of His promises and definitely needed them at that time. **James 1:5 says, "If any of you lacks wisdom, he should ask God who gives generously to all without finding fault, and it will be given to him. (NIV)".** And **1 Thessalonians 5:24 says, "The one who calls you is faithful and he will do it" (NIV).** For the situation we found ourselves in, you can't beat promises like these. And you know what? In His wonderful grace, He kept them both.

Now Jon had been studying and organizing the Murle language for over four years and he was a good teacher who had studied not only their language but had also studied their culture as an anthropologist. So, he taught us the language along with the culture, which was probably the best language and orientation we had ever had in our missionary career even though it was the shortest. We took good notes and immediately started putting them to use. This is always the best way to learn a new language: Use it. There were unlimited opportunities to use it since the number of Murle who knew any English at all was almost zero.

Every morning before our class began, there would be a few patients coming into our backyard, mostly mothers and children. Jon or Barbara or their house worker, Lamon (Lah-moun), helped us until we began to learn the words for symptoms and treatments. So even before the six weeks were completed, Ginny and I and Gwen were doing fairly well with the most frequently used medical terms.

Since Jon was going to start the Bible translation on his return after one year, he had done a lot of work on Christian and biblical vocabulary. We wrote all these biblical words Jon told us, because we knew after the Arensens left Pibor it would be difficult to find them. We used those notes we had taken every day.

MURLE RELIGIOUS CONCEPTS

We learned from Jon (and later from our own experience) that the Murle had some rather disorganized religious concepts. They had some pantheistic beliefs that certain pools in the rivers, certain big trees, and a small stone mountain near Pibor had supernatural significance or were places where sacrifices could be made to influence their lives or future. They didn't seem to have the great fear of the spirits of departed ancestors of the people in rural Zimbabwe and other East African tribes. They did obtain charms from some of their traditional medicine women, which seemed to us to be more to ward off bad luck or illness than to deter evil spirits, as we had seen in other places in Africa.

A SAD GOOD-BYE

About four weeks into our language study, we had to say good-bye to Cathy, since it was time for her school to start in Kenya. All three of our children had gone to boarding school in Ethiopia after the third grade. (Ginny home schooled them through the third grade.) Because their school was in Ethiopia where we were serving, it was in driving distance. But this good-bye was much harder for us since she was our youngest and now was having to fly by herself to another country and go through customs, etc., all on her own. We knew she was in good hands with the AIM (Africa Inland Mission) flying service, and the mission school she was attending, Rift Valley Academy, was also operated by AIM. Still, it was difficult to tell her good-bye that day at the Pibor airstrip. In all of these uncertainties, however, we were learning to trust the Lord with our own lives, a completely new ministry and also with the lives of our children.

On our way back to Africa a few months before, we had gone through the new experience of leaving our two boys, Mike and Stan, in the US for college. We had to tell them good-bye in a strange airport in Florida, knowing they would have to make their way back to Texas on their own. Another truth we relied on during our whole mission career was this: "If we, as God's servants, are in the center of His will for our lives, then we know He will take care of our children wherever they are." Not that there wouldn't be dangers for them and times of separation and sometimes seemingly insurmountable problems, but we believed our loving Heavenly Father would walk us through whatever happened and He would take care of us and our children. Also, if something came up and we needed to be there for or with them, then we would be there. They knew and believed this. It made separation possible.

ON OUR OWN

Finally, that fateful day came when the SIL airplane was due for the dreaded departure of the Arensens. Of course, we were the ones who dreaded the day. The Arensens were joyful to be going home to see family and friends after finishing their latest tour in Africa. We dreaded the day because we had leaned heavily on Jon and Barb as teachers and interpreters, both of language and culture, when we didn't understand either the words or actions of the people around us. They also knew all the local officials and understood Sudanese government policy in a way that would take us a long time to grasp.

We all accompanied them to the airstrip across the river that morning with apprehensive hearts. Shortly, we heard the plane motor in the distance and then it came into view and landed. Even though the airstrip was adjacent to the Sudanese army camp, the army was not very reliable in caring for such rural and remote airstrips, because a government plane rarely came to Pibor. So, we always went early to the airstrip when a plane was due and cleared away anything on the airstrip that might cause a problem for the pilot, like animals or rocks. A kind of third world "do it yourself" airstrip maintenance program.

Any time a plane went to such a remote station as Pibor, the missions always tried to help those who were so isolated and never let such a plane go empty, if possible. So, even though ACROSS usually sent the AIM air service planes for its people, we knew our mail and maybe some other food items would be on that plane for us. Even though we were sad to see the Arensens leave, we were glad for the anticipated replenishing of our supplies and we always welcomed the mail.

When the plane taxied to a stop, we unloaded our station supplies and then began loading the Arensens' seemingly few things. On small planes in the bush, due to weight restrictions, a family of four is allowed precious little weight for luggage, so one has to plan ahead and send most of their belongings ahead, when a plane was returning light. Then they would collect those things sent ahead before they left for wherever they were going.

Our airstrip at Pibor

As the pilot was warming up the engine, we were waving another sad good-bye, when Ginny glanced at the supplies that had come on the plane. There with our things was the box of literacy books. These books would be the key for teaching the Murle to read in their own language so they could read the Bible when it was translated. Also, these books, written mostly by Barb, were really their main contribution to the work at Pibor up to that time. Jon had told us they were coming on the plane that was carrying them away for one year.

Now Ginny had been very interested in teaching literacy from early in our missionary career and had started in our early years in Zimbabwe. We didn't realize at the time the significance of this one question she shouted above the noise of the plane engine that day: "Can I test these literacy books while you are gone?"

They shouted back, "Use them any way you can!"

You will see how God used that little exchange later, but it was a significant step toward making disciples among the Murle.

GOD'S BACK-UP POWER PLAN

Now, let us go back and fill in another gap that has a great bearing on all that happened in our lives and ministry among the Murle. Our last years in Ethiopia, especially during the arrest and incarceration by the Communist government, had convinced us we needed a group of prayer warriors, who would pray regularly for us and for our ministry. When we left Ethiopia there were about sixty of these people praying for us and for those we were ministering to. During the eighteen months in Kenya and our six months of home leave before going to Sudan, the number grew to be over 100 people who were concerned and praying for us and the Murle.

When we first enlisted these prayer warriors, we informed them we were going to write them every month and share specific prayer requests, but also, we expected them to write us and share their prayer requests from their lives and ministries. We knew this would be difficult for us because the plane didn't always come every two weeks. We knew it would also be difficult for them, but felt that if they were committed to pray for us, then we needed to be committed to pray for them. We had learned in the discipleship principles we had studied that the keyword in "discipleship" was "discipline." God would require it of us and also of our prayer partners.

We knew if we were obedient and they were also, He would bless His ministry among the Murle as they prayed for us, and also bless them as we prayed for them.

We had to be tough sometimes when we didn't hear from one of them for two or three months. We would drop them off our mailing list until they wrote to say they wanted to join the prayer partner band again. We were embarrassed a couple of times when they wrote that they had been in the hospital or ill for several months.

All the above to say that we are convinced all of us need some prayer partners who we pray for and who pray for us regularly, and with whom we communicate often and mutually share our needs and victories. Our experience at Pibor convinced us that God is just waiting for us to ask, so He can show His power and keep His many promises about prayer. **(Matt. 18:19; John 14:13, 14; John 16:24; Mark 11:24; Phil. 4:6,7; 1 John 5:14,15)** Why did He make such broad, sweeping promises if He did not plan to bless immensely those who would believe them and be obedient to just "ask" Him?

Before we went to Pibor, one of our prayer partners wrote to say the Lord had laid on her heart to claim **Acts 4: 29,30** for us and for our ministry in Sudan. This passage was in the apostles' prayer when they were being threatened by the Jewish rulers, and it says, "**Now, Lord, consider their threats and enable your servants to speak your word with great boldness. While You stretch out your hand to heal and perform miraculous signs and wonders through the name of your holy servant Jesus.**" When we received that word from her, we were greatly encouraged because we knew the Lord frequently spoke to us through them. We passed that promise to all our group of prayer warriors for them to also claim concerning the ministry at Pibor.

That promise had come several weeks before we left the US and before we had any idea what an impossible situation we were to be in among the Murle. After arriving at Pibor and coming face-to-face with the realities of life there, we were at a total loss as to how to begin making disciples. With our meager knowledge of their language and even less understanding of their culture, although Jon had done his best, we did not know how to begin. Our prayer was, "Lord we don't know where to start. We believe You have brought us here and You have shown us plainly that Your plan for winning the world is for us to make disciples, who in turn will make other disciples. But, Lord, it is going to take a miracle!"

CHAPTER 3

The First Miracle

MORE PATIENTS

We may have let the promise from Acts be pushed back in our memories by the seemingly impossible circumstances around us, but the Lord doesn't even let circumstances enter into the equation when He is in control. In the few days after Jon and Barb and their children flew away from Pibor, patients continued to come every day. I treated them in our back yard while we started the big task of cleaning up the old hospital building. Most of the patients were mothers with children, but there was the occasional adult patient with malaria, even though the rainy season was only beginning. Some people have it lurking in their systems and it will break out when their resistance is lowered by another problem like a viral infection or GI upset.

First clinic outside our house

THE OLD HOSPITAL

The old hospital was structurally fine because it was made of cement block, and miracle of miracles, it still had a good corrugated iron roof. I had decided I would fix up the front two adjoining rooms and make them an outpatient clinic and minor surgery, hoping my surgical cases would be mostly "minor." The building was about thirty feet wide and about sixty feet long. Amazingly, the ceilings in most of the rooms were also still in place. I designated the next two rooms as treatment rooms (without beds) for any male and or female patients who needed prolonged treatment. I didn't need beds because the Murle live very simply in houses made mostly of straw and mud. They sleep on kob skins, so if they had to spend the night in the old hospital, they would bring their kob skins to sleep on.

The next two or three rooms, we used as storerooms. One feature of this building was that it had a long veranda from front to back and the upper part of this veranda was not enclosed above the height of the walls and ceiling. As you stood on the veranda, you were just looking up into the attic above the rooms. When I looked up the first time, I was startled to see a giraffe skeleton – a skull on a long bony neck, looking down at me out of the attic. One of the missionaries in the past had a good sense of humor and had patiently wired all this together. For over twenty years, it had stood the test of time. It was so well done it could easily have been displayed in a museum in London or Washington, DC.

After the missionaries left Pibor, the building had not been used but had just sat there empty. Birds built their nests in it and animals must have wandered in and out, so it was a very dirty place. But the Murle had never destroyed or dismantled any part of it. Maybe they too enjoyed the joke of the giraffe looking down out of the attic, because they had not harmed it in any way. Also, maybe some of the Christians had hoped against hope during the long civil war that this building would again be used to help those who were sick and injured. If so, God had answered their prayers.

BADLY TIMED EMERGENCY

However, just as we were about to get the clinic in order, a serious patient came one morning. We, of course, could not have known the significance of this one patient, whom God was going to use in a wonderful way to open doors for making disciples among the Murle. Her name was Ngatiin (Ngah-teen) and she only lived about a mile from us. Due to our recent arrival, the trust level toward us was still very low. She had been ill for about three days before coming, and her history was vomiting, a gradually distending and painful abdomen, and no bowel movements since it all began. From her history, I had almost made a diagnosis before examining her. It seemed obvious she had a bowel obstruction. I had seen many of them in Ethiopia. Those who had survived required surgery, but a few refused surgical care under any circumstances, and they all died.

Now, I am not a trained surgeon, but bush doctors on the mission field have to do a lot of things they aren't trained for. I was able to do colostomies. I would open the abdomen, cut the colon proximal to the obstruction and bring the end of the colon through the abdominal wall to relieve the pressure. I did this on those who were agreeable, to save their lives. In Ethiopia we had sent them to Addis Ababa, the capital city, for a surgeon to do the definitive work in anastomosing the bowel and closing the colostomy. I knew I would have to admit her to one of the rooms set aside for patients who stayed overnight.

LADY WITH BOWEL OBSTRUCTION

Here at Pibor we had several problems that made surgery seem a bad option. At that time, we didn't have an operating table. (Several months later we spotted one outside a building at the army camp, and with much begging persuaded them to "loan" it to us. They had no use for it and never asked for its return.) Also, I had merely swept out a room for Ngatiin to put her kob -skin bed while we began antibiotic and fluid therapy. The next morning, I contacted ACROSS in Juba and asked about transferring her to the Juba hospital. To my dismay, they informed me that whatever we could do for her at Pibor would be better treatment than she could receive in Juba. That was rather unbelievable, since it was the regional hospital, but after a few more months in Sudan, we realized their assessment was, in fact, correct.

Our next problem was that I didn't have anything but local anesthesia. We were under the mistaken impression at first that we could send surgical patients to Juba, and I had not brought any general anesthesia. We tried to get ACROSS to locate some spinal anesthesia in Juba, but they again had zero results. Having only arrived, I was very limited in all my medical supplies and had planned to order IV fluids, etc., after setting up the clinic. It is amazing how emergencies never wait for the ideal time. But we had a very good supply of re-hydration fluid (little packets of sugar-salt-mineral mixture furnished by UNICEF) that could be given orally. After a couple of days, I found that Ngatiin evidently had a very low obstruction and could take very frequent small amounts of this fluid without vomiting. This was good news, but of course not real good news, because one cannot live on re-hydration fluid for a very long period.

PRAYER IS FAILING – "DO SOMETHING"

Here was our first serious patient and she was obviously going to die without surgery (which seemed out of the question) or a miracle. So, we decided to pray for a miracle. At first, we got together with the Haspels and prayed two to three days with seemingly no results. Ngatiin was alive because of the re-hydration fluid keeping her hydrated, but she was still distended and in pain. She could keep nothing down but the re-hydration fluid. So, about the seventh day, we got more desperate and got out our Bibles and read the **fifth chapter** of James, starting with verse 14. It says: "Is any one of you sick? He should call the elders of the church to pray over him and anoint him with oil in the name of the Lord. And the prayer offered in faith will make the sick person well; the Lord will raise him up. If he has sinned, he will be forgiven. Therefore confess your sins to each other and pray for each other so that you may be healed. The prayer of a righteous man is powerful and effective." So, we used this passage like a cook book recipe to claim healing for Ngatiin.

There was a church at Pibor, although in the years since the first civil war it had lost much of its vitality due to lack of spiritual teaching. The last missionaries had left prior to 1964 and there was no complete Bible or New Testament to help the Christians grow spiritually. We were informed, however, there were some elders in this church. In desperation, we called on them to be obedient to this passage. We explained about the verses in James and told them we wanted to pray together with them for Ngatiin.

At that time, there was no Murle translation of the book of James. In fact, there were only poor translations of three books: the gospel of John, Acts, and Romans, which had been done many years before and had not been checked adequately either grammatically or linguistically. There was a local pastor who understood some English but was not trained and probably didn't know this passage in James. So, John and I tried to explain the passage to the him and these elders as best we could in simple English and our poor Murle. We took some salad oil from our house for anointing, and then we all went over to the old hospital building. We anointed Ngatiin with the oil and got on our knees to pray for her. John and I prayed in English and did our best to confess our sins as the passage required. However, the three church elders and pastor prayed in Murle, and we didn't know what they prayed. We hoped they understood about confessing their sins. All we knew was that for the next three days, Ngatiin's condition remained the same.

ANOTHER PRAYER

So, on the night of the tenth day, I couldn't sleep. Most of us American doctors believe in action, that is, "doing something." In fact, "doing anything" rather than "doing nothing" when a patient is thought to be dying. Due to this work ethic from our culture, deep down, even we Christian doctors believe that just praying is almost "doing nothing." So, I had this guilty feeling that I wasn't doing enough for Ngatiin, although I knew surgery would be next to impossible and probably fatal, considering the condition under which we would have to work.

That night I wrestled with this dilemma for an hour or two, and then I woke up Ginny. Sometimes being married to a mission doctor has its disadvantages, especially in the middle of the night.

I said, "Honey, I can't sleep thinking about Ngatiin over there dying. I have decided that if God doesn't heal her by tomorrow, I'm going to have to operate. Would you pray for her with me one more time?"

I have thought about it since, and have decided that it was sort of a veiled threat to God. The threat was, "If You don't heal Ngatiin, I'm going to really mess things up tomorrow."

All I knew to do was a colostomy, with no hope of definitive surgery to close it. Any self-respecting Murle woman who only wore a loincloth would rather be dead than have a permanent colostomy. Also, I would have to do it under local anesthesia, which I had never done, and wasn't sure *could be done*. I would have to do it without an operating table, probably on the floor, which I had never done either. To keep a sterile field under those circumstances would be hopeless. But I felt I had to "do something"! Ginny knew I was desperate, so she kindly spent a comforting time with me in prayer and then we were both able to go back to sleep.

MY OTHER JOB

Before the Arensens left, I had volunteered to help out two mornings a week in the government clinic in Pibor town. There was a Sudanese male nurse in charge there and his supplies, equipment, and medicines were almost non-existent. The two days I went over there, I took my own examining equipment and had to refer many of the patients to our afternoon clinic at the old hospital for medications. The morning after that fateful middle of the night prayer and my decision to "operate" if God didn't heal Ngatiin was my morning to work in the government clinic. I went by the old hospital building to check on her before I walked the one-and-a-half miles to the clinic in town.

I was hoping with all my heart that she would be jumping around like the fellow in Acts chapter 3 who was miraculously healed by the Lord through Peter and John. But alas, there she was, still lying on her back, her abdomen still very distended and still in much pain. In my very limited Murle, I tried to explain what I planned to do to "help" her that afternoon when I returned from the government clinic. I'm sure she understood very little of what I was trying to say, but probably in her trusting way she knew I cared and wanted to

help. What could a simple uneducated Murle person understand about abdominal surgery?

So, I went on to a miserable three to four hours at the
government clinic. I usually saw forty to fifty patients each
morning there. While I was seeing the patients, all I could
think about was how I was going to do this procedure under
local anesthetic, or how to do it without an operating table,
or how to keep the field sterile, etc., etc. As I said, it was a
long and miserable morning, and when I finished, I started
my trek back home. Since the hospital building was on the
way, I stopped by to talk to Ngatiin one more time. Being a
Murle, she did not understand anything about surgery, so
I felt I should try to explain once again what was going to
happen, or at least what I hoped might happen.

GOD KEEPS HIS PROMISE

So, I approached the door with dread, knowing I probably could not muster enough Murle to explain anything
adequately, especially abdominal surgery to a simple Murle
woman. **But when i stepped through the doorway, I could
not believe my eyes.** Ngatiin was sitting up and her distention was gone. She was smiling and told me after I left that
morning, she began to feel much better. She had passed
some flatus and then some stool and her distention disap-
peared and the pain was gone. I listened to her abdomen,
and for the first time in ten days, I heard some bowel sounds.
Instead of her, it was I who wanted to jump up and down!
God had given that scripture to our prayer partner and now
He had kept His word in Acts 4:29 and **"had stretched out
His hand to heal and to perform miraculous signs and
wonders through the name of His holy servant, Jesus."**

Ngatiin began to eat and drink normally and only stayed another two days at the clinic. She went home and never had symptoms of a bowel obstruction again. Now, I must say that for a medical doctor, this was a fantastic miracle, but for Ngatiin, it probably wasn't that big a deal. She didn't know the medical facts I knew. Before God intervened, she was at death's door! As a Murle woman, all she knew was that she was very sick and now she was well. The Murle people frequently get sick and then get well – **but we knew** and God had confirmed to us that He was "in control" and was working out His plan for this tribe. Although we didn't realize it at the time, this was the beginning of disciple making among the Murle. I will let Ginny tell you how it all came about, since the Lord definitely spoke to her heart at that time with a further revelation.

CHAPTER 4

Ginny's Literacy Class

<u>Ginny's speaking.</u>

Ginny's Story

While Ngatiin was recovering, and we were continuing to pray for her, God seemed to speak to my heart and say, "I had a purpose in healing her. I want you to teach her how to read using the literacy books that came in on that airplane." That was a big order for me, because I certainly had not mastered the Murle language and I wondered how in the world I could teach anyone to read a language I couldn't even speak or understand. But Sam and I had learned, when God speaks, you obey.

So, I called Lamon, the one who spoke halting English, and asked him to interpret my conversation with Ngatiin. Maria, her sister-in-law, was with her when I asked her if she would like to learn to read Murle. Of course, me being the wife of the doctor who made her well (she thought), (we know that God healed her) she would have agreed to anything. I waited a week before I took the book to her house because I wanted her to feel well enough to study. I figured if I went to her, she would show up for class, but if I asked her to come to me, she might have other things to do and wouldn't be regular.

That first day when I got to her house to begin our class, there were four other people there who wanted to learn to read also.

A Murle house That was exciting because I knew when there was more than one studying there would be competition and it would sharpen them all. However, after showing them the book we would use that day, I realized I would have to do some preliminary work before I could really use the literacy book Barb had written. God gave me a wonderful answer as I prayed for wisdom on how to begin teaching them.

THE PLAN GOD GAVE

I took Lamon with me and we went out to their compound the next day. I asked them to listen to the sound I was going to say and then for them to tell me what the sound reminded them of. Then I proceeded to sound out all the letters of the alphabet, omitting the vowels, because they would have to be learned by memorization. For example, the phonic sound for "b" (when repeated over and over quickly) sounded like their porridge bubbling on the fire. The "f" sound was like a cat spitting at a dog. Lamon told me what they said for each letter and I wrote it all down. I took home all the things they had told me and had my artistic husband draw on small individual flash cards a small picture of each sound. Then beside each picture I drew the letter it represented. After teaching them all the letters on these cards, I then could teach them to read phonetically. Because I used the sounds they were familiar with from their culture for the consonants, they learned the vowel sounds very quickly. When they had mastered the consonants and vowels, then it was easy for them to put them together to make words. After words, came the book. They could read.

LITERACY WORK BEGAN

I went out to their village every morning, carrying a walking stick and claiming **Luke 10:19, which says, "I have given you authority to trample on snakes and scorpions and to overcome all the power of the enemy; nothing will harm you."** That was **my** verse the whole time I was in Sudan, because I was walking those trails for the two-and-a-half years we were there. I never once saw a snake on the path, although there were many cobras around. I knew God was taking care of me. I did meet two drunk soldiers one day on the path. When they tried to detain me, I was pretty afraid, but I remembered and quoted my verse, and they let me pass.

But back to my story. I spent the entire morning in class, six days a week. Our classroom was a round house made of young, cut tree trunks driven into the ground in the shape of a circle, with a thatched roof. If anyone had lived in the house, the cracks between the tree trunks would have been filled with cow dung and mud. But because no one was living in that house, there were big cracks all around us. It was really better though, because this let in the breeze, when it was blowing. It was so hot there.

We didn't have chairs and a table for our class, mainly because they didn't use chairs and tables. Their chairs were kob skins, their tables were kob skins, their beds were kob skins, their suitcases were kob skins, which they rolled up and carried on their heads when they had to move. They were able to roll up all their earthly possessions in these skins as they started their trek to find water when the river dried up. So, we sat on these skins each day for class.

We began our class with prayer, and one day during the prayer time, I felt something biting my "seater." I peeped down to see what was biting me and saw I was sitting in the way of a long line of army ants who had chosen to pass through that house. I was in their path and didn't seem to be moving, so they attacked me so I would move. Needless to say, the prayer was broken up as I moved out of the house quickly.

Another day while I was teaching, I noticed something move up over me in the grass of the thatched roof. I stopped teaching and looked more closely, and there was a snake slithering right over my head. I do hate snakes, so I fled outside again and refused to return until they got the snake down. They assured me it was a harmless kind and wouldn't hurt us, but I was not persuaded. It took a while to get the thing down. It liked being there in the cool roof among the grass. Finally, after succeeding in getting it down, we began our class again.

One habit the Murle had that "grossed me out" was the way they blew their noses. In class, they blew it into their fingers, reached behind them and smeared it up and down on the wall, which was a tree trunk. It made me sick at first, but I guess you can get used to anything. They had never seen a Kleenex or a handkerchief. Because they wore such few clothes, when it was cooler at night they often had bad colds, so this happened a lot. There are some things in our culture, like Kleenex, that are very nice.

Because the Murle language was written phonetically, I could read the book but didn't know what the words meant. They thought I knew what I was reading. As time went on, I began to learn the meaning of these words. I did teach them to read, but they helped me to learn Murle. I was highly motivated to learn their language and did better in this language than any of the other ones I had studied. I realized out there that motivation is the key to language learning. People who are "talkers" usually learn to speak a language better than quiet people. I am a quiet person, but I had Jesus' message to communicate and I wanted to learn Murle. And I did.

MY FAITHFUL CLASS

The Murle are a nomadic tribe who move with their cows. When the rivers dry up and the grass is all gone, they have to take their herds to find water. So, one morning I went to their village and everyone had packed up and left the previous day. My class refused to go with the group and faithfully came each day to study. It was not until the next year that it dawned on me that they had chosen to go hungry to study with me after their families left them. I knew that Maria's husband came in every so often, to bring them meat if he had killed a kob, but I had no idea how hungry they must have been in between those times. I feel quite humbled and yet honored that they felt learning to read was worth being hungry. I am sure I wouldn't have done that to learn anything.

Soon after we began studying, my class began to tell me about this boy who lived nearby, who wanted to learn to read too. He was paralyzed from his waist down from polio he had contracted as a child. His mother had brought him to Sam for treatment a month or so before this, but of course, there was nothing Sam could do for him. His mom had built a little hut for them; she and the boy, Mama, had been there in our vicinity ever since. (In English, Mama is an unusual name, but that was his name). I knew who this boy was, because every morning on my way to class he greeted me from his hut near the path. I spoke to him but didn't stop to visit with him. I really tried to ignore him, because I just didn't have time to teach him too, and I knew he wanted to learn to read.

I knew he couldn't come to class because he couldn't walk. If I taught him, it meant I would have to go to his home to teach him. I spent every morning from 8am to noon with Ngatiin and the others, rushed home, threw some lunch on the table, and dashed to the clinic to do the nursing for Sam all afternoon, until after dark on many days. I did not have a spare minute to go to this lad's home to teach him.

I told the class I was sorry, but I was doing all I could possibly do. About every other day they reminded me of Mama and how much he wanted to learn, so I really felt bad about ignoring him and refusing to teach him.

So, one day, I let class out early and walked by his hut to speak to him. I discovered someone from our class had been going over to his hut each day, sharing with him what they were learning, and Mama already knew a lot. I realized I would have to teach this lad. (He must have been sixteen or seventeen by then.) So, I started going by Mama's hut each day after reading with my class. Mama was very motivated and he learned very quickly. It was a joy to teach him. He soon became my star pupil. The others in the class were so happy for him.

"Mama"

After everyone mastered the reading, I then began a Bible class. There was a poor Murle Bible translation of a few books written in the English orthography. (There was also the same volume in the Arabic orthography – but that was useless to us.) I used this poor translation, but I had to do a lot of explanation because most of the time this translation was very difficult for them to understand.

All of my class became believers. By this time the others in their families, who left with their herds, had returned home. Since the rains had come the river was full of water once again. My class began to teach the others about Jesus and before long, others had become believers in Jesus also. Every night we could hear them from our home, singing, and we knew they were also praying for their neighbors. **Eternal Fruit.**

There was no electricity at Pibor, so when night came the only thing they could do was sit in the moonlight and talk, tell stories, or sing. So, it was natural that now, after they became believers, they would meet, sing, and pray together. They did this every night. It was so much nicer than hearing the drums beating and the chanting we had heard early on. We never really knew what all the drums at night meant.

After a while, these new believers wanted to build a church outside the walls of the village compound where they lived and kept their animals at night. They all worked together to cut the trees, and grass to thatch the roof.

Church built by the Murle believers The Murle wrote their own songs, using verses from the Bible and their own music. So, there were new songs being sung almost every week. Different people led the services since there was no pastor for that church. Living at Pibor was a real challenge, but a wonderful time spent watching the Lord work in the lives and hearts of lots of people. **Eternal Fruit.**

After my class became believers, I started going with them to visit their neighbors to witness to them. There were some in almost every home we visited who believed. Finally, the ladies told me it would be better if I didn't go with them anymore. They said the people were simply saying they were believers to please me, and it would be better if I just let them go and do the witnessing. They told me they knew their neighbors and now I had taught them how to witness to them. They felt like they would know who was truly repenting of their sins and who wasn't. So, I stopped going with them.

The Lord performed a miracle to heal Ngatiin, but He had even greater miracles in mind. Through Ngatiin He began a spiritual ministry that would reach many in the whole Murle tribe. Ngatiin is part of our **Eternal Fruit**!

CHAPTER 5

Rainy Season

CLAIMING RAIN, SHOWERS, AND BLESSINGS

The Lord had showed His great power by healing Ngatiin and had heard our prayers and let the trucks arrive safely with our household goods and also those of the Bodenhamers (who were to arrive at Pibor later). So, Ginny and I, the Haspels, and some of the church elders began to pray in earnest for rain. We knew these Christians were not mature and wanted them to see they could call on God to meet all their needs. This kind of faith is essential for true disciples and we wanted to see true disciples among the Murle.

Now, we had read that this part of Sudan had a rainfall of sixteen inches per year, so we felt we should at least ask God to give us this amount. We had been told the past year there had been very little rain. We had a rain gauge, so we were going to measure the Lord's response in a scientific way. We wouldn't want to say we were going to check up on God, but I guess you could say we wanted to see how He was faithful to answer our prayers.

As we communicated regularly with our prayer partners in the US, we told them about our prayers for rain with the Murle and asked them to pray along with us. We also wanted them to see God's faithfulness. The Murle had seen how dismal their crops had been the previous year and how they and their livestock had suffered, so we wanted them to see what God would do when His people prayed.

Shortly after the trucks left some more good rains began to fall. However, there were not any concentrated rains, like we expected. We always want something really dramatic. So, we continued to pray with the church elders and asked God for a good rainy season. We knew the Murle wouldn't understand about sixteen inches average rainfall or what that even meant, so we missionaries kept that part between ourselves and our prayer partners in the USA.

The rains continued rather sporadically and there were several weeks without any rain.

During that time, ACROSS was able to take advantage of this lull to send another truck with several drums of fuel, which we needed very badly. We would need diesel fuel (for the Land Rover), gasoline (for John Haspel's truck and our small generator), kerosene for the fridges and freezer, etc. The plane could bring propane as needed for cooking, but we needed this other fuel. So, we were very glad for this dry spell, even though we were praying for rain. Even though the rains had been sporadic, actually they had been very nice for the crops and the grazing grass.

About halfway through the rainy season, the church elders felt the Lord had answered our prayers because the river began to flow, but was rising slowly, and the country was transformed from brown to green. And to a certain extent they were right, because the Lord was meeting their needs and the needs of their cattle and that was their main concern. But we still had our sights on sixteen inches of rain during that rainy season. Normally the rainy season continued through the month of September, but we had specifically prayed that sixteen inches of rain would fall by September 30th.

MORE WORKERS IN THE HARVEST FIELD

Finally, the Bodenhamers received a work a permit. Wasting no time, they quickly came to Pibor by plane. We were glad to see them and praised the Lord for their safe arrival. The wide plain was now impassable for vehicles. Their household goods had come with ours and their crates were at their house, ready to be unpacked. Because of the Lord's miraculous and timely provision of the truckload of building materials, we had finished most of the repairs on their house. This family would make a great contribution to our Pibor team because Ron was an agriculturist and Judy was a medical laboratory technician.

Ron would help in the community development and agricultural projects and Judy would make a great contribution in our medical ministry. I was seeing lots of patients, day after day, but was really not able to make many definite diagnoses without an x-ray or any kind of laboratory examinations. It is possible to treat lots of patients without lab work, and I had been doing it for a few months and most of my past medical career – nine years in Zimbabwe and nine years in Ethiopia. But as any doctor would testify, it is much easier when some definite tests can be made to pinpoint some specific disease or illness.

The Lord is good to call just the right laborers into His harvest fields. That is what He said He would do in **Matthew 9:38** when He said, **"Ask the Lord of the harvest, therefore, to send out workers into His harvest field."** Of course, that was doubly true of Ron and Judy, because one of Ron's major interests, being an agriculturist, was a good harvest. They had three children: Jeff, age sixteen; Keith, age eleven; and Tammy, age two. They shortly began to study the Murle language, but they were at a great disadvantage because the Arensens were still in the USA and the Haspels and we were very unenlightened and poor language teachers. However, we tried to teach them as best we could, using the notes Jon had left us.

PLANNED HUNGER

Now the Murle are a pastoral people, and as we have already said, semi-nomadic, in that they travel with their herds, but only when all the grass is depleted near their homes and the rivers are dry. However, they also planted small fields of sorghum maize to furnish food during the rains. We were hoping Ron could help them improve their yield of grain and also help develop some other crops that would improve their nutrition. Those were *our ideas* and we found out later the Murle were not as interested in these ideas as we were.

After we learned their language better, they explained to us that they purposely only planted small plots of grain because if they planted and harvested a big supply of grain (or even other food crops), many of their lazy relatives (and everyone has some of these) would come and camp out at their houses and stay till it was all eaten. It would be contrary to their culture to refuse them. So, every family planted and harvested a minimal amount of grain and pumpkins, usually just enough for their families to last for a few months after the harvest.

Because of this cultural quirk, they just planned to be hungry for the two months after their food was finished and the following month while their pumpkins matured. Since the pumpkin leaves were also edible, they were eaten for two or three weeks while the pumpkins grew. Of course, they were waiting also for the kob migration to come through Pibor, so they could have meat. It is hard for us in Western society to imagine such subsistence living. We found this was the life cycle of the Murle and hunger for a few months was just part of it. In our society, where three meals a day is normal, to even miss a meal or two is a great sacrifice.

This was brought home to us at a mission conference on one of our early home leaves from the mission field. We had been learning about fasting and believed this was another way to grow spiritually if we spent quality time with the Lord. We wanted to grow spiritually, so we had begun to fast from time to time. At this mission conference, we saw that the ladies of the churches were spending all their time in the kitchen and missing the spiritual food of the conference. Therefore, we suggested that we just fast each day at lunch time so the ladies could join us and receive spiritual food too. We thought that would be good for us all and especially for the ladies who were missing out on the meeting. This idea was shot down like an enemy aircraft. No one even wanted to consider it. American Christians are great on planning banquets, but rather weak in observing fasts.

Not only were the Murle willing to go hungry, but when they did eat out of desperation and severe hunger, what did they eat? During the first months of hunger in the Murle life cycle before the rains, they were in "cattle camps," twenty to thirty miles from Pibor. In these camps, which were near some available grass and where water was closer to the surface, usually in dry river beds, they dug down (sometimes ten to fifteen feet) to get water for themselves and their cattle.

Sometimes they were fortunate enough to find a stray group of kob that had left the big herd and were attracted by the grass. Of course, armed only with their spears, they were not able to kill many, usually only one at a time, but it was enough for the whole group at the camp. They had learned also about some wild roots and some wild leafy plants that were edible. So, they gathered these and cooked them for food, and they only ate one meal a day.

They were able to milk their cows, but only after they had calved, because they were not primary milk cows. When they got really hungry, they mixed the cow's milk and blood for food. (I call this a bloodcurdling diet.) How did they do this? They had learned to nick the large vein in the neck of their cattle, bleed about a pint of blood from the animal, and then mix it with the milk. Then they would put pressure on the vein until the bleeding stopped. This was, despite being totally unacceptable and nauseating to folks like us, a very nutritious drink.

TRAVEL ON THE RIVER

Jon Arensen had a small aluminum fishing boat with an outboard motor, which he generously left for us to use during the rainy season. We were very glad for that, because when the plane came, crossing the river became impossible without it, except by wading up to our waist (later up to our necks). Most of the time we put the boat (without the motor) on top of the Land Rover, drove the one-and-a-half miles from our houses to the river crossing, rowed across the river, and walked the other half mile to the airstrip. If we had been notified on the radio that there were heavy items on the plane, we took a wheelbarrow with us. When we needed to visit villages that were more than one or two miles away, we used the boat and motor and traveled by the rivers at that season.

The boat we used to go to the airport

A FAMILY AGAIN

Our two sons, Mike and Stan, planned to come visit us during their summer vacation. Mike had just finished his third year at LeTourneau College in Longview, Texas, working on a business and aviation degree, and Stan had finished his freshman year at Hardin Simmons University, at Abilene,

Texas, studying geology. (Each time one of them arrived we would get out the boat to cross the river to meet them.) The boys came to Pibor in June and Cathy was able to come for a month starting the last week in July. It was wonderful for a few weeks to be a family again. Even though we were on the back side of nowhere, Ginny had collected ingredients for each of their favorite dishes, which included Mexican food, pecan pie, etc. etc. We had brought many kinds of seeds with us and had planted a garden almost immediately when the rains started. So, along with all of the favorite dishes, we had lots of fresh vegetables – including lettuce, tomatoes, carrots, squash, black-eyed peas, and green beans. It seemed that everything grew well there – when there was rain.

We had many hours of visiting and catching up on their lives since our last time together. Our kids became older cousins to the Haspels and Bodenhamer children, and they all seemed to get along well. Cathy had decided by that time that she was going to be a nurse, so she helped in the clinic much of the time while on vacation. When we had surgical cases, which we did in the mornings (on days that I didn't go to the Pibor government clinic), she and Gwen Haspels teamed up and helped. Ginny did all the nursing at all the afternoon clinics after her literacy classes in the mornings. She left the surgery to Gwen and Cathy. All in all, we were like a big family and things were so peaceful – for a short while.

CHAPTER 6

Soldiers And Gunfire

UNWELCOMED EXCITEMENT

With the rain and the transformation of the whole landscape from dusty brown to verdant green, the good fellowship with our children, the family atmosphere – things went smoothly for the rest of the year.

Not So!

Our enemy seems to have violence simmering just beneath the surface no matter where we are in the world, despite the blessings God may be giving to His children. We believed the rains, the good crops, the grass, the flowing river, and the green all around us were due to the Lord's graciousness and in direct answer to the prayers of His people for rain both in Pibor and the many prayer partners scattered around the world. (Many of our prayer supporters were also missionaries in other countries.) But the peace we were enjoying was soon to be shattered.

First, we heard some rumors there was unrest and quarreling between the Murle and the Sudanese police and army personnel living at Pibor. All of these army men were from different Sudanese tribes and from other parts of Southern Sudan. A week or so went by and nothing seemed to come of it, so we relaxed again.

While we were in Ethiopia from 1974 – 1977, we lived through a Communist coup, a civil war, our arrest, and my two-week imprisonment. Since these events in Sudan took place in 1980, only three years had elapsed since those terrible times in Ethiopia. All that had happened there was still fresh in all our minds. We all, children included, remembered those tense days as I waited to be released from detention.

We found out in Ethiopia that it is impossible to be neutral in a civil war. In our first country, I had tried my best to remain neutral by treating any and all patients who came to our clinics, whether government or rebel. I found that *both* sides accused me of disloyalty and partiality, and instead of making friends of both sides, I made enemies.

So here we were at Pibor, Sudan, with tensions rising again. We hoped against hope that those reports truly were rumors, so we could enjoy the peace we had experienced in the past weeks. Ginny's literacy students were doing fabulously, and clinic attendance was good. Also, we were becoming a little more proficient in the language. As the patients told their symptoms we could understand without having them repeat too many times. Also, in a halting way we were able to give a short Christian witness before every clinic and pray with the patients in halting Murle. Most of all, we were developing relationships with the Murle people and we knew that was essential, if we were to make disciples. Would we ever become free enough in the language, both in understanding and speaking, to actually make some real disciples? With trouble brewing, could it actually happen?

Oh yes, it could, because even in the face of troubles and uncertainty, the God who called us to Pibor was still in control. All we had to do was put ourselves in His hands and trust Him no matter how bad the circumstances seemed to be. Since it was His plan for us to make disciples, it would happen despite all the conflicting circumstances. Of course, it is easier for us in hindsight to see this, but at that time our faith was sorely tested.

In the book of Job, we learn God sometimes allows Satan to test those who put their trust in Him, but we must always realize God is ultimately in control. If you will remember, Satan couldn't test Job without God's permission. We believed this was true in our lives as well. And in the last chapters of Job, we saw that God turned it all around and blessed Job more than he could ever have imagined.

Through our experiences in Ethiopia, we realized even in dark days and wondering if God was really in control, He always was. After our experience there, we also saw that out of trials, God can bless in remarkable ways. While trouble seemed to be brewing in Pibor, we were glad later that we had been through tough times before, and knew that **Romans 8:28** is **always** true. It says, **"And we know that in all things God works for the good of those who love Him, who have been called according to His purpose."** But Romans 8:29 explains why this is true. It says, **"For those God foreknew he also predestined to be conformed to the likeness of his Son, that he might be the firstborn among many brothers."**

God deliberately lets trials and troubles come into the lives of those He loves and who are committed to Him, so He can turn them around and let them work out for good.

In the process, He molds us into the image of His Son Jesus. Troubles do come to all of us, but God has a wonderful purpose in all of them.

When we heard gunfire coming from the direction of Pibor town, our worst fears were validated. We kept hoping this trouble would blow over without escalating, but in another few days, there was more gunfire and we heard that the Murle warriors (all the young men) were getting ready for a fight.

Of course, the army and police had guns and the Murle only had spears, so it seemed hopeless for the Murle side. The clinic attendance dwindled to a trickle and there was almost no traffic of people walking back and forth to Pibor town on the main path that went by our house. We found the trees in our yard were tall enough for someone standing on the top branches to see all the way to town. So, our son Stan, who loved to climb trees, climbed to the top and watched every time we heard gunfire or rumors of activity in that direction.

After another day or so, the shooting started and continued. Stan started to climb, but we could tell the firing was getting closer, so he decided to wait. It continued to get closer and then we heard bullets hitting the limbs of the trees in our yard. We didn't know what was going on, but since the firing continued in intensity and was gradually getting closer, we all decided to sit on the floor behind the three-foot stone walls. That was the safest place in the house, since above those walls there was nothing but screen wire, and bullets could freely pass through screens.

We, as a family, couldn't believe this was happening. We said, "Lord, we thought we left this kind of stuff behind in Ethiopia, but now it is happening again!" We remembered those years of anxiety as hatred and bloodshed erupted all around us. So, as we sat on the floor behind those three-foot walls, those dreadful memories returned to all of us.

As a doctor, these times always brought a sense of more responsibility and a question about my own ability to help people with serious wounds. I also remembered in Ethiopia that the Lord had always given me His wisdom when mine was lacking, so I just prayed for His peace and wisdom in the midst of turmoil. There was nothing any of us could do but pray, so in prayer, we put our lives in the hands of the Lord. We didn't know what was going on, but we knew He did.

ARMY VISITORS

Soon the firing tapered off and then it stopped. All was quiet, but we could hear people walking around outside, and then there was a knock on our door. I went to the door, and when I opened it, there was the commandant of the army camp in town. Standing behind him were ten to fifteen soldiers, all with rifles. He knew English and said the radio at the camp was not working and he wanted to use our radio to notify headquarters in Juba of the trouble in the district.

We lived on the Murle side of the river and we really wanted to remain neutral and not be associated with the army, but what can you do with armed soldiers requesting to use your radio? Well, we did have a solution that day. ACROSS only had one scheduled time a day to pass messages by radio, and that was at 7:00 in the morning. Our radio had only one fixed frequency, so it was impossible for the soldiers to call their headquarters on their frequency. We convinced the commandant of this and told him that if he wanted to talk to ACROSS headquarters in Juba in the morning, he would be welcome to pass a message.

Actually, we didn't feel he would want to pass such sensitive information through foreigners, so we were almost sure we would not have this request again. He was polite and thanked us, and his men did an about face and headed back to Pibor town. Immediately they resumed firing and continued firing all the way back to town. Then we realized what was going on. All of that barrage was to scare the Murle, in case there were some around. They had not been firing at anyone in particular the whole day.

THE FIGHTING ESCALATES

After another few days, we heard gunfire in the other direction, but it was at a greater distance. This time we decided not to panic, but kept our ears open. We chose to stay inside until it settled down, but it continued sporadically for another hour or so.

Finally, I said, "I don't know where the shooting is, but it seems still in the distance. I'm going outside and pick some beans for supper."

Cathy said, "I'm going with you. I'm tired of being cooped up in the house!"

So, Cathy and I went outside to the garden about twenty yards from the house. As we picked the beans, the firing continued. However, now that we were outside, it became apparent it was gradually getting closer. We were determined that we were going to pick the beans, shooting or no shooting. However, in the next ten minutes the intensity of the firing increased and soon it was obvious the noise was getting very close. We quickly lost our resolve to pick those beans and ran for the house.

By now the firing was very loud, very close, and continued unabated. We joined Ginny and the boys seated on the floor behind the stone walls and wondered what was going on. We could tell that whoever was playing shoot-out was passing our house on one of the nearby paths. There was no evidence that any of their bullets were hitting our house or were even near our house. However, as they passed, the firing continued, but we could hear no return fire even though we expected it, because these folks were headed toward town where the army and police posts were located. When we thought it safe, we went outside to try to identify the noise makers, but we could not see them for the trees and bushes.

We heard the next day that the Murle warriors had over-run a rural police station and had stolen some of the rifles. However, all of this shooting was from the policemen who had escaped with a few rifles and lots of ammunition. Again, they were not shooting at anyone, but were using scare tactics to keep the Murle warriors away while they made their way to Pibor town. We knew they had succeeded in scaring us, but we didn't know how much fear they put into the Murle.

THE FIRST OF THE WOUNDED

In the next days, tensions continued to rise, with reports of clashes between the Murle and the police in the other rural police posts. In fact, in a short time most of the rural police posts were closed. I was amazed that I had not seen wounded people up to this point, but one day I was called to town by the police to see a patient who had been wounded.

My heart sank when I was taken to the patient who was literally in a cage in the middle of town. The cage was similar to ones holding animals in zoos. There was no roof on the cage, and I found out the patient had been there for three days. It turns out that he was an eighteen-year-old young Murle, named Chiliyu, who was deaf and dumb.

He was found by the police in a house in Pibor. When they opened the door and ordered him out, he couldn't hear or reply to them. So, they shot him in the lower leg and then dragged him to this place. He had been locked in this cage for three days. Because of their anger with the Murle warriors and their hatred for the Murle, they were merciless with this young man. In fact, I wondered if they had given him food and water to drink because he was lying in the hot sun, since there was no shelter over him.

I didn't know why they had sent for me, except maybe some of the Murle people who lived in the town had asked that he be seen by the doctor. Of course, the wound with the bones exposed was badly infected. There are some fractures of this part of the leg that don't heal well, even without infection or exposed bones, and even when treated by orthopedic surgeons in the USA. The circulation in the lower third of the leg is known to be poor and is the cause of many so-called "non-unions" of fractures, even in the best of conditions.

The police probably realized they had made a big mistake by shooting this young man, so when I demanded that he be released to me for treatment, they acquiesced and I brought him to the clinic. By that time, I had the operating table from the military commander and had acquired some spinal anesthesia. But I hadn't foreseen amputation, so I didn't have a bone saw.

However, in Ethiopia on one occasion, I was called on to do an amputation at a rural clinic site, and one of the school-teachers in that place had furnished a hacksaw blade that had served well after we sterilized it. So, we gave this boy lots of antibiotics that night, then the next morning sterilized my hacksaw blade and performed an amputation on Chiliyu's leg about mid-calf.

We were able to show God's love to him in the midst of the suspicion and hatred engulfing the whole district at that time. When his family came, they could communicate with him with their own private sign language and we tried to share with him and them how much God loved them. He healed quickly and was making his way around soon with the aid of a walking stick – a short pole that he clutched with both hands and used as a crutch. His family was very grateful. They had seen many people with such wounds die because of the infection. We claimed **Romans 8:28 again – where God says, "all things work together for good for those who love God and are called according to His purpose."**

Some readers may be saying that all these activities don't seem to be related to disciple making, and we felt the same way at the time. However, through our experiences at Pibor, we found our main tools for making disciples was a willing-ness to spend time with people, to teach them God's word and to show God's love to them by our lives, day by day. Someone has said that random acts of kindness can speak louder than all of our many words. Also, it has been said that discipleship is "caught" as much as taught. **Eternal Fruit.**

We knew we didn't plan any of the things that had hap-pened – Ngatiin's healing and the subsequent literacy classes (especially the hunger experienced by those first disciples in the literacy classes), the good rainy season, the war between the Murle and the army and police, Chiliyu's healing, etc. – we just trusted that the God who had let them all happen would use them to make disciples and enlarge His kingdom in Murle-land. We were learning that discipleship and disciple making was more of a lifestyle than an organized plan of study. Of course, if we had read the scriptures with more understanding, we would have seen that this has been true since New Testament times.

Who could have planned for Peter and John to meet the crippled man at the temple in **Acts 3:22?** Jesus must have passed by that man many times because he was over forty years old, and according to the scriptures had been placed at the temple gate every day. Then in God's time, he was miraculously healed thorough Peter and John's bold testimony. Only God makes plans like that.

All through the book of Acts, there are records of persecution of believers as well as being beaten and stoned. Believers were falsely accused but also had been miraculously released. There had been healings, supernatural visions, and extraordinary answers to prayer, etc., that no human being could have devised. We like to think about and preach about the miraculous deliverances, the supernatural visions, and extraordinary answers to prayers, etc., but we don't like to think about or preach about the suffering part of discipleship. However, the end result of all of God's divine working, both the good and seemingly bad, was that disciples were made and strengthened, churches established and the gospel was preached all over the known world.

How did much of the New Testament get written? God let one of His choicest and most obedient servants, Paul, get falsely accused and locked up in prison for several years so he could write those wonderful discipleship letters God uses in our lives today. God has used these letters throughout history to strengthen His church. If Paul had not been in prison, he would have preached all of those wonderful truths to the churches of his day, but they probably would never have been written down.

Did God actually let Paul be locked up in prison and suffer like that? We have to believe He did. Then He turned it around and worked it out for good, so the church through the ages would be blessed by what God Himself said through Paul. We don't like to think about it, but suffering just goes along with being a child of God. And in that case, it is <u>not bad,</u> because anything that brings us closer to God is **always** good. We like the first part of **Romans 8:17,** but don't like to think about the meaning of the second part. <u>**"Now if we are children, then we are heirs – heirs of God and co-heirs with Christ, if indeed we share in His suffering in order that we may also share in His glory."**</u> We like the idea of being a co-heir with Christ, but the fact that He says we must suffer with Him frightens us.

A long time ago, at the end of our first term in Rhodesia, a little child coughed in my face and I developed a severe eye infection. For six months I had terrible pain in my left eye and the end result was that I lost the sight in that eye. As I was suffering through all those months of pain and discouragement, the Lord seemed to be saying to me, "Pain and suffering are not **bad**, because they cause you to trust Me more, and anything that draws you to Me is actually **good**." After that, I told folks God closed one of my eyes so I could see better. In fact, the one good eye He left me was better than most people's two eyes. For the rest of my medical career there seemed to be no significant limitation because of having only one eye. And the spiritual truths He taught Ginny and me during that time truly opened our spiritual eyes in many ways that nothing else could have done.

So many of the things that come into our lives are things we don't plan. But when we stop complaining and realize God is truly in control of our lives, then we can submit to His plan for us. He has a master plan that is perfect, and His plan for us is to mold us into the image of His Son. We saw Him do things at Pibor that we could never have planned, and we praise Him for His great work among the Murle. We realize now that many times it was *in spite of* us and not *because of* us. Even in the seemingly bad things, He could and did turn them around and worked them out for good.

MURDER BY HATRED

Chiliyu was the first war victim, but there were others. A few days later the police brought another patient who saddened my heart and caused us to realize the extent of the injustice and the depth of the hatred in the hearts of those in conflict.

This Murle man had been found in a field near the town and near the army camp. Possibly there had been some orders for Murle men to keep their distance, but probably this man had just innocently approached the town and was accosted by these soldiers. They beat him with sticks and kept beating him until he was unconscious and also unrecognizable.

Some of his Murle friends either called the police or took him to the police. The local police were different from the soldiers. Of course, the police were powerless to accuse the army, so they just brought the patient to me and hoped I could help the poor man.

He was still unconscious and had many lacerations on his scalp. He was bleeding from his nose and ears as well as from all the lacerations. I spent a long time trying to suture the lacerations and we tried to console the family until late evening, but it was to no avail because the man died despite all our efforts. As a doctor and as one who had come to Pibor Post to minister to the Murle, I was angry, discouraged and also depressed at the injustices we were seeing. It seemed to us that this animosity was never going to end. It was so unfair in our minds to see the army, with all the weapons at their disposal, intimidating and now blatantly killing some of the Murle tribesmen who only had spears to defend themselves.

I took a chance as a missionary and as a foreign national and wrote a stinging report to the civilian Administrator of Pibor. I stated the man had been murdered by the army and his death should be investigated. I knew at the time that it would have little effect, but it helped me somewhat to express my indignation. Nevertheless, for several days I was very depressed and Ginny expressed in one of her letters home that I just "plodded around" during that time. We were wondering if we could ever minister in an effective way under such conditions. For all we knew, this might go on for months. It truly was a depressing time in all our lives.

Things had started in such a wonderful way at Pibor and we had seen God work in so many miraculous ways. I didn't realize I had taken my eyes off my Lord and had started looking at circumstances. I had forgotten Romans 8:28 and the knowledge that God can take even the worst circumstances and turn them around and work them out for good. I had preached that truth many times to others, but now I was failing to apply it in my own life. Isn't that true so many times in our lives as Christians? But of course, through such times God teaches us to truly trust Him. So, we just kept on learning. And there were more lessons on the way!

ANOTHER MIRACLE

I have mentioned there was fighting between the Murle warriors and the police in some of the rural outposts. About a week after one of the clashes, a seriously injured Murle man, named Nyati, was brought to me. He had been shot in the left shoulder by the police and had been left by them to die. His friends had rescued Nyati and hid him for a week in fear of being accused of harboring a wanted man. Finally, they brought him to our clinic. When I examined him, I was sure he could not survive. The bullet had gone through the upper part of his shoulder, destroying the brachial plexus nerves. He would always have a paralyzed left arm due to the loss of these essential nerves. Worse, the bullet had also taken off the upper part of his left lung.

In the week he had spent without treatment, that lung had collapsed, had become very badly infected, and a big cavity in his left chest became half-filled with foul-smelling, purulent fluid. I couldn't believe the man had even lived a week. He must have lost much blood initially, but how could he have survived with so much infection and only one lung?

I didn't know what to do. I had never seen any injury like this. I knew he needed antibiotics, of course, but I would have liked to also put antibiotics in the chest cavity. I realized that would take all the antibiotics in my storeroom for just one patient and leave none for anyone else for the next several months. Yet I knew I must try something.

So, I resorted to an antiquated local treatment for wounds. I had lots of the purple powder called Gentian Violet that we used often in Africa for thrush in children and occasionally for superficial skin infections. In the old days even in the US, this treatment was used for superficial skin infections, but in our sophistication, we American doctors shied away from it because of the purple color. GV (as we called it) had antibacterial as well as anti-fungal qualities. Since I had lots of roll gauze bandages (sent by some churches), I soaked several of these in a Gentian Violet solution. Then, as gently as possible, I stuffed them into his chest cavity until it was full.

I put him on oral antibiotics and told him to come back in two days, but I really didn't expect him to live to return. **But I was very surprised.** He not only came back in two days, but kept coming back every two days for a couple of weeks. Each time, it took less of the roll gauze to perform the treatment, and each time he was stronger than the last. Then I changed it to twice weekly and later once weekly. I would never have believed it, but after four months his wound was completely healed.

He only had one lung and only one useful arm, but I felt the Lord had performed another miracle right before our eyes. Of course, this was very encouraging, and the depression I had suffered the past few days was replaced with a new faith, knowing that God was truly in control and could be trusted with circumstances surrounding us.

BLUB, BLUB, BLUB IN THE NIGHT

Many of the Murle people in our immediate vicinity became very frightened because of the violence going on around us. We don't know how the thought came to them, but one day they decided it would be safer around our house than in their villages. Maybe they thought the police and army wouldn't shoot at a foreigner's house like they might do at theirs. Whatever their thoughts might have been, some men came and asked us if they could bring their families and camp out around our house for a few days. So, what could we say? We agreed, but didn't realize what it would be like to be surrounded by a lot of Murle for a few days.

First of all, we found we would get very little sleep. It seemed they slept in shifts (not the kind ladies wear) because there were people talking all during the night. Also, they built fires to cook their food, and when the wind changed all the smoke blew right through our screened windows.

Besides all that, several of them smoked water pipes. These are made of gourds and have water in the bottom of the gourd. The tobacco is in a little clay cup that sits on top of a small reed tube that allows the smoke to be drawn through the water. So, it was *blub, blub, blub*, pause, *blub, blub, blub* the entire night as they passed the pipes from person to person. So, the second day we decided to set some rules and declared some strict guidelines if they wanted to sleep around our house.

First, they must put their cooking fires a good distance from the house and only have small fires after dark. Second, pipe smoking would only be tolerated on the periphery of the compound, instead of just outside our bedroom. Also, talking must be done in very low tones along the outer fences. The next nights were more tolerable, but during the days we were under close Murle scrutiny.

By this I mean that living in our house was sort of like living in an aquarium and they enjoyed the entertainment of gawking at the strange life of these white foreigners. The

Lord was merciful, and after four days the tension eased and they felt they could return to their villages. We had learned a lot, and probably they had learned even more.

DIFFICULT GOOD-BYES

Our two boys had booked their return flight for the middle of August, and as much as we hated to see them leave (especially with all of the fighting around us), we knew they had to go and get on with their education. They also were apprehensive for us, not wanting to leave their mom and dad and sister in obvious danger. As we prayed about it, Ginny, Cathy and I felt peace about staying and letting them go.

Our family has claimed the promise of **Colossians 3:15** often in times of hard decisions, and the Lord provided His peace when we most needed it. In the Amplified Bible that verse says: **"And let the peace (soul harmony which comes) from Christ rule (act as umpire continually) in your hearts (deciding and settling with finality all questions that arise in your minds in that peaceful state]) to which as (members of Christ's) one body you were also called (to live). And be thankful (appreciative), giving praise to God always."** In our experience, we have found that no matter what the circumstances are, if the Lord gives His "peace" in our hearts, we **know** everything will be totally in His hands and the end result will bring blessings to Him.

With all the tension in the air, we realized we had to make sure our lines of communication were open with the army commander in Pibor when we were expecting a plane. So, we made several trips to inform him about our plans to bring the AIM mission plane on the day Mike and Stan were to leave. Our first trip convinced us this was the right procedure, because we found the army had dug foxholes and had machine gun emplacements about every twenty yards down both sides of the air strip. It looked like they were expecting an invasion. Since their problem was with the Murle, who only had spears, we couldn't understand what threat may come from the air, but they were prepared to defend Pibor from any aggressive threats from hostile aircraft. We tried to think who might want to annex Pibor and the Murle, but we couldn't think of any country who would want this poor area with all of its problems. The soldiers were so edgy, we could see them shooting up any plane that came in unannounced.

Fortunately, the day came and the plane landed without any serious consequences. With lots of lingering hugs all around, we put the boys on board and said good-bye. These times are the hardest in every missionary's life, telling our children good-bye. We know in our hearts these young people have to grow up and be on their own, but when we live 7,000 miles away without any good way to communicate, it makes departures very, very difficult.

That day, we knew in our hearts that the all-powerful, all-knowing God who called us to such places had given us these children, and His promise in **Philippians 4:19** included them too: **"And my God will meet all your needs according to his glorious riches in Christ Jesus."** We had claimed this promise many times in our lives, so now we claimed it for our two boys again, as well. After the plane took off Ginny, Cathy and I returned home to a house that felt very empty. There were feelings of loss and nostalgia all our hearts.

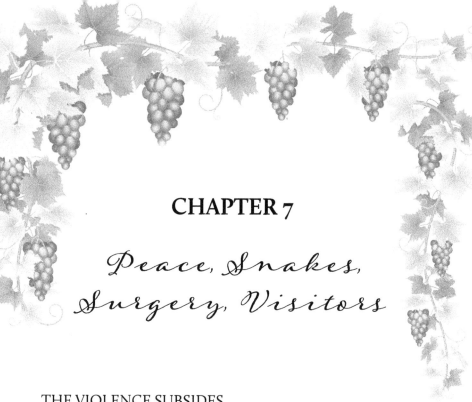

CHAPTER 7

Peace, Snakes, Surgery, Visitors

THE VIOLENCE SUBSIDES

After the boys left in the airplane, we continued to pray the conflicts between the Murle warriors and the Sudanese police and army forces would subside. As you can imagine, the Bodenhamers, Haspels, and we had many prayer meetings with each other and also with our Murle Christian friends. We asked the Lord to let peace return to Pibor. He heard us.

One day a large army helicopter flew into Pibor. There was a high army officer on it from the Northern Sudanese government and also some Arabic troops. Somehow, the troubles at Pibor had been reported and the officer and troops were sent to investigate. The commandant at the army camp was of another Sudanese tribe that had much animosity against the Murle. He had been allowing the persecution of the Murle by the local soldiers. After investigating, it was determined that there would be no peace at Pibor as long as that commandant remained in charge. Therefore, the commandant was replaced by another one who understood the situation. At that change, things began to settle down and peace really did return to Pibor. We were very thankful and praised the Lord. Our lives began to return to a more normal routine. But we still missed our boys, who seemed to always have something new going on.

Since the Murle didn't keep chickens, early on we decided we needed to start a flock. So, we had some hens and a rooster flown in from Kenya. They were a great help to us with their eggs and even some good ole fried chicken on special occasions. We even let a hen or two set on their eggs so we could increase our flock. Right before Mike and Stan left, one of our hens hatched a brood of chicks, so we now had baby chickens. One day a hawk swooped down and carried off one of the chicks. That prompted us to build a small coop (and also gave the boys something to keep them occupied) to protect the hen and chicks from hawks during the day.

But another day before the boys went back to school, while we were eating lunch, we heard the mother hen clucking wildly. When we looked out to see what was wrong, we saw a large monitor lizard out there, trying to break into her cage. It must have come up from the river, then squeezed under the fence around our house. Mike and Stan jumped up, rushed out of the house and on their way, picked up sticks to chase the lizard away. It was about the size of a medium-size crocodile, but when it saw the boys coming, it began to run. Well, in the heat of the chase it had forgotten where it had come in and this proved to be its undoing. The boys were huffing and puffing and sweating profusely, but they kept running after the lizard. At the end of the chase, the chicken thief's career was ended.

Another day while Ginny was standing by the stove cooking, she looked down and there was a snake slithering toward her. She screamed, of course, and that brought Stan running to see what was wrong. Ginny had climbed up on the card table (our dining table), trying to get as far away from it as she could. Stan, being the brave son that he was, rescued his mom by killing the snake. That was the only time we saw a snake on our side of the house.

Because Mike had killed a kob with a spear during the kob migration, our meat supply while the boys were with us was adequate. After they left, however, we returned to buying meat from the Murle warriors.

Sam grinding kob meat for our hamburgers. This is also where we hid from bullets. These warriors had continued to follow the migration and were able to bring us meat from time to time. This helped us and also helped them to have cash to buy salt, sugar and occasionally a piece of cloth for their wives to throw over their shoulders. They had few needs for money, however, unless their cooking pot sprang a leak and they needed to buy a new one.

ANOTHER SNAKE IN OUR HOUSE

One night when John was on a trip for their mission, Gwen, his wife, knocked on our door in the middle of the night. We felt sure she had a real emergency, like one of their children was sick. When we opened the door, she told us in a loud whisper she thought she had a snake under her bed. Rustling noises in some papers she knew were under her bed had awakened her. She said she was too scared to get down to look. She hadn't wanted to make a lot of noise either, because her children were asleep nearby. She wanted me to come. As I hurried by, I grabbed some unused wooden two-by-fours standing by the door to Cathy's new room that had just been built.

Turning on the flashlights, I looked under the bed and saw some movement inside the newspapers. I decided I would have to pull the bed out if I was going to kill that snake, which turned out to be a cobra. With Gwen's help, I pulled the bed about a foot out from the wall. I climbed up on it and shone the light down. The cobra was very cooperative, because just at that moment it stuck its head out of the papers. I quickly brought the two-by-four down on its head and held it there until I was sure it was dead. When we got the papers out of the way, we had about a four-foot cobra there in the bedroom. None of us had any idea how it got into the house, but needless to say, we were very careful to firmly close all the doors when we went in and out of the house from then on.

AN OUTSIDE SNAKE

Cobras were probably the most common snakes there at Pibor. An evening later, we found another one outside about the same size. It was between our part of the house and the Haspels' dining room. You remember our house was shaped like an "E." They lived in three sections and we lived in two. So, we had it trapped with three walls surrounding it. I was able to kill it with a large stick. These snakes were the factor that caused Ginny to claim **Luke 10:19** every time she went to teach her literacy class.

THE BEST SNAKE STORY

One evening while Ngatiin was so sick, the elders came to the Haspels' home to pray for her healing. I joined them as they sat around the Haspels' dining table. During the prayer, I opened my eyes and saw a small snake slithering between the feet under the table, heading right toward me. I didn't want to break up the prayer meeting but needed to decide something quick before the snake got to me. I decided the best thing to do was to put my foot down on its head when it got close to me. I had on a terrycloth pair of open-toed bedroom slippers and prayed my foot would hit the head of the snake. Remember I just had one eye and my depth perception was not good. God was with me and I hit the snake right on its head. I kept pressing down hard until the prayer meeting was over.

Then in a quiet voice I said, "Everyone, move away from the table because I have my foot on a small snake."

Everyone jumped away and I raised my foot.

The elders yelled, "Black Mamba." John grabbed something and killed the snake. We were all happy it was dead and John was very glad to get it out of his house.

GOOD NEWS

During the rainy season, our communication with the outside world was by radio with the ACROSS office every morning. We were cut off because the road on the flat plain was under water, but the airplanes could still come. On that particular morning, they told us on the radio our boys had arrived safely in Nairobi, Kenya, and then flew on to the USA. We knew they were traveling together and God was looking out for them. Cathy really did miss them, though.

SURGICAL CASES INCREASE

At the clinic, since we saw outpatients all afternoon, I reserved the mornings for surgeries (mostly minor). However, there were only four mornings available, since I went to the government clinic two mornings each week. In the beginning, the minor surgeries consisted mainly of superficial skin cases, like the removal of keloid tumors from earlobes. A keloid tumor actually consists of scar tissue that continues to enlarge after the original cut or abrasion has healed. They are more likely to form when there has been an infection in the wound. Also, they seem more likely to form on dark skin.

The Murle did all of their piercing of ear lobes, lips and tattoos under very unsterile conditions, so many keloids formed on those places. The keloids in the earlobes seemed to be the largest and were the most troublesome to them.

Many times, if I could remove them under sterile conditions (which I did), they did not return.

I also found many cases of entropion of the eyelids due to scarring from a disease called Trachoma. This scarring caused the eyelashes to turn under and brush on the cornea every time they blinked their eyes. This was very painful, but also destroyed their corneas and gradually caused blindness. In Ethiopia, I had learned to do a minor surgical procedure under local anesthesia. This operation returned the eyelashes to their normal position and the pain would be gone. Also, the patient wouldn't go blind. It was a wonderful operation. Many days, after the news spread throughout the tribe, our surgery consisted of six to eight of these on the days we did surgery. It only took fifteen to twenty minutes to do one.

Sam at the clinic getting ready for eye surgery

Before Cathy had to return to school, another serious surgical case came in that she never forgot. A family brought in an older teenage boy who had been bitten on his leg by a snake about a week before. Probably it was from a puff adder, since it was on the lower leg and seemed to be very tissue toxic. (Puff adder bites caused much local tissue toxicity, whereas cobra bites had some neurotoxin factor and caused death more frequently than the puff adder.)

Why they waited so long to bring him, I don't know, but the leg was in very bad shape. This was obvious by the appearance of the leg, but more obvious from the smell. From the mid-calf down it was gangrenous. I knew we would have to amputate his leg to save his life. I started him on antibiotics that afternoon and sterilized our instruments, including our trusted hacksaw blade. That was all I had to cut bone.

The next morning, Gwen Haspels and I scrubbed up for the surgery and Cathy was our circulating nurse. The one-legged spinal anesthesia worked very well and the operation went well until the time to throw away the part of the leg that had been removed. Cathy was the only one who was not scrubbed, so she got to take the leg outside away from the clinic. Gwen and I were very sorry for her because it really was a nasty smelling job. From that day on, when I asked her to help with surgery, I had to assure her it would not be cutting off any part of the body.

That young man healed, and despite all of the infection, even the stump healed nicely too. Because of the good result, Cathy was also happy and we all praised the Lord the boy was okay and able to return to his home.

A WET AIRSTRIP AND ANOTHER GOOD-BYE

After the boys left, we still missed them, but our fellowship with Cathy was special. Toward the end of August, our hearts again began to be heavy, because she too would be leaving with Jeff Bodenhamer for their boarding school (RVA) in Kenya very soon. Mentally, we knew God was taking care of them, but it was always heartrending to have to tell them good-bye after one of their visits. However, God always met the needs of our heavy hearts. We knew Cathy needed her education and needed to be with her peers at school. But knowing these things without a doubt still didn't take away the pain of separation when the time came.

Early the morning of departure, ACROSS came on the radio to tell us a different plane would be coming for the kids. It would be a MAF (Missionary Aviation Fellowship) plane from Malakal, an MAF base north of us on the Nile River. Shortly after talking on the radio, we had a heavy downpour of rain. On any other day that would have been a very welcome event, but on the day a plane was coming, this was actually bad news.

Our airstrip was a dirt strip with a little grass on it, but not a thick grass cover that would have helped to support an airplane. Later that morning, we got a message from MAF saying they were sending a two-engine plane and it would have three passengers already on it. This meant the plane would be heavier because of the two engines and also because of the passengers. We went over to the airstrip to check it out and found it was very soft from the rain. But sometimes the bush planes had large balloon tires that were adapted to soft, muddy airstrips.

We had told the army commandant the plane was coming, so there was no problem from the army about the plane landing that day. We hoped against hope it would be able to land and take off with the children and the other passengers.

At the appointed time, we went back to the airstrip with the children and their luggage. Soon we could see the plane approaching and our hearts sank. It was a two-engine plane as they had said, but it **didn't** have the large balloon tires we had hoped for. It had small wheels and small tires that planes used for landing on asphalt airstrips. We didn't know what would happen, hoped for the best and began to pray they would land safely. It came in and did very well as it touched down, but as it slowed to taxi, the small wheels sank into the soft soil and soon it was hopelessly stuck.

Since there were some places on the airstrip that were firmer, we all helped to push the plane to one of those spots. When our kids got on board, the pilot went to the end of the airstrip to turn around for his takeoff. He was hopeful he could get the plane quickly off the ground. He tried to get up enough speed before hitting the soft spot where he got stuck, but he just couldn't. He tried several more times that day and then gave up.

LOTS OF COMPANY

So, we had the pilot and the other passengers (a missionary and two other students going back to RVA) for an overnight visit with us at Pibor. Fortunately, missionaries and their kids are very flexible, so we improvised for bedding and managed to feed them all. Judy Bodenhamer had fixed a big, good-bye meal of Mexican food for Jeff before he left, so we fed them the leftovers and it was adequate for everyone. Southerners always overcook!

The next morning, the pilot woke up very sick with nausea and vomiting. He was sick all that day, so we had many house guests again for another night. When you are as far out in the bush as we were, it is actually very nice to have guests from time to time, even if they are unexpected.

The third morning the pilot was feeling much better, so very early we took everyone back to the airstrip (which had dried by then) and we knew again God was at work, because the plane had no trouble on takeoff. It had been quite scary the first day when the pilot had tried to get the plane into the air. But that day, with no trouble on takeoff, he flew them all to Juba and then the next day all the kids were able to fly on to Kenya and to school.

After the plane left, with heavy hearts we walked with the Bodenhamers back to the river, rowed in our boat across the river to our car, and returned to our empty nest. The Bodenhamers still had two children at home though, so their nest wasn't empty like ours. Still, we knew we were where God had placed us.

WHAT ABOUT THE SIXTEEN INCHES OF RAIN?

When Cathy went back to school at the end of August, the rainy season was coming to an end, but we had only recorded fifteen inches of rain. The book we had read that recorded rainfall for our area had said the rainy season was to last until the end of September. We had asked the Lord for at least sixteen inches because we wanted Him to demonstrate His power for the Murle. Fifteen inches was the average and we were asking for one inch more. The end of September came and we had recorded just a tad over fifteen inches. We were disappointed.

I have said before that the Murle only planted one grain crop for each family, which was a small plot of millet. So, in late October, they harvested their millet and it was a good crop. Our Lord is so good, and many times does the unexpected when we don't even ask Him. We had not had enough faith to ask for any more rain after the end of September. But would you believe? A nice, hard rain came in early November, completely out of season. The Murle had only chopped off the millet stalks close to the roots, so it began to sprout again, and in early December another good rain came. That brought the total rainfall to over sixteen inches and the millet stalks actually grew a second crop. This was wonderful.

Sometimes the Lord answers our prayers super abundantly, far over and above what we can ask or even think. Also, sometime when we think He is not going to answer our prayers, He answers them on His timetable and the answer is much better than we had asked for. I am sure He would like to do much more for us, but we are afraid to ask Him. He is waiting on us to ask. I wonder if He ever gets tired of waiting on us to ask Him for big or even small things. We think, probably He does.

CHAPTER 8

A Murle Custom And Confession

DEATH ON THE COMPOUND—A FRIGHTENING MYSTERY

One day that fall, we were shocked when the Murle pastor of the Pibor town church came to inform us that some people had died in our compound but we, who lived there, were totally unaware of the event. I think he came to tell us about this because he thought we needed to know about it.

There was a rather large building about twenty to thirty yards down the path from the old hospital building where I had our daily clinics. Since it was past the clinic, we rarely ever walked over to it. Occasionally some of the Murle would ask if they could stay in this empty building. It had probably been used at one time in the 1950s as a storeroom by the Presbyterian mission. It was a large, rectangular, empty building about forty feet by fifty feet in size. However, it still had a good roof and when cleaned up, it provided good shelter for folks in need.

Two or three weeks before the pastor shocked us with his announcement, a Murle family had come by, needing a place to stay. We told them they could stay in that building. They had said two of them had diarrhea and I gave them medicine, but they did not return to the clinic or report back to me. So, when I didn't see them again, I assumed they had regained their health and had continued their journey to their village.

Now, at this time, we didn't know about the Murle burial customs, or lack of them, but we found out from the pastor that it is not their custom to bury the dead at all. When someone dies, they just drag the body out of their hut into the forest to the "west" of their compound. The east is, in the Murle tradition, more sacred than the west, since they believe God created the first human beings to the east. And, of course, if most biblical scholars are right, the Garden of Eden would have been to the east of Pibor.

Evidently, two of the people in this family had died and the others were afraid to approach us, since we were actually strangers to them. So, they had quietly dragged the bodies out to the west of this building and had left secretly. We feel they were probably afraid we would report the deaths to the police, who might accuse them in some way. At any rate, some people had discovered what was left of the bodies and reported it to the pastor. He, in turn, had come to report it to us.

We were shocked, to say the least, that people had died on the fringe of our compound, and for whatever reason they had been afraid to tell us. As a doctor, I could imagine their deaths could have been prevented if we had known. There were many shocking things in our lives during those early learning days at Pibor, and this revelation concerning the Murle traditional "last rites for the dead" was one of the most shocking. Jon Arensen had tried to teach us as many of the Murle customs as he could recall, but he had forgotten to mention this one. So, we made up our minds not to be surprised in the future at any new revelations that might arise out of our work among this people.

MAYBE A SOLUTION

A few months later in early 1981, we got some other patients with severe diarrhea. Since by that time Judy Bodenhamer had our "bush" lab in operation, we tried to diagnose these in a more scientific manner. However, all she could find was an overwhelming infestation of a parasite worm call Strongyloides stercoralis, commonly known as "threadworm." Since we had an abundant supply of worm medicine and this parasite was normally relatively easy to treat, I felt the treatment would be simple and easy. We were wrong.

Despite the treatment, which we tried for several times on the same patient, the diarrhea continued and this certain patient continued to get weaker. Along with the worm medicine, I tried IV solutions for hydration, and added antibiotics, just in case we had somehow missed a bacterial infection. Despite everything we did concerning treatment, the patient died after several days.

In another few weeks, we had a similar patient with an overwhelming parasitic infestation. We tried every treatment that we could think of, but this patient also died. Up until that time, I was of the opinion no one ever actually died from a parasitic infestation. Of course, there was no way we would ever know, but it was about this time in history that the first AIDS patients were being diagnosed in Africa. One of the first peak geographical areas in the AIDS epidemic was Uganda, which borders Sudan to the south. So, it is very possible we were seeing some of the first cases of AIDS in Sudan. Many AIDS patients, because of their impaired immune systems, develop overwhelming infestations of parasites and have severe diarrhea that is resistant to treatment. However, this was before we knew of any reported cases of AIDS, so we didn't have any way to suspect this could be a new disease of some sort.

Again, if it had been AIDS, it seems we would have had a continued epidemic of such cases, but we didn't. I am so grateful we didn't. It will always remain a mystery as to what caused those deaths. Despite Murle customs to the contrary, we insisted that the patients who died in our care be buried. This was not offensive to the families of the patient, and in fact, they seemed pleased that we were willing to do this. As we thought about it later, they had no way to dig a grave because none of them had a shovel or any such tool to dig with. So maybe their custom had evolved because they had no way of doing anything differently.

SURPRISE FROM OUR DOG SUGAR

Our shocks did not end with just **learning** about the Murle burial practices. Late one evening as we were talking to some of our Murle friends on the path in front of our house, we looked up to a horrifying sight! Our dog, Sugar, was coming down the path, carrying a human skull that still had a little skin on it. When she got to us, she politely dropped it down at our feet. Our Murle friends were as dumbfounded and embarrassed as we were. What do you say at such a time as that? So, they just excused themselves and made their way to their homes. Sugar, I am sure, thought she had found something new and exciting. We had a laugh at her expense after we got in the house. But we did take the skull and bury it. We presume it was the skull of one of the bodies that had been discovered by the townspeople in the woods near our compound.

FLIES AND A LION

As the year progressed, the rivers all dried up and the sun seemed to get hotter every day. The crowds continued to come to the clinics in great numbers. At the same time, it seemed the number of flies increased exponentially in the clinic, because every Murle who came through the clinic's door brought in a multitude of flies on their backs. Every hour or so we would spray the flies (naturally with a perfumed bug spray), trying to keep them off of us and our medicines. By the end of the day, the clinic floor was black with all the dead flies.

Sugar chose to follow us to the clinic every afternoon. She was a Boxer and looked ferocious to the Murle. They were very afraid of her, even though she was very friendly and gentle. We tried to convince them of this, but to them she looked like a small lion. They even called her a "maa," which means *lion* in Murle. When she came to the clinic, she would lie down under my examining table and go to sleep. Because she was asleep, the Murle didn't seem to mind her being there.

One day when we had seen the last patient, Ginny and I hurried home because we were exhausted. We hadn't been used to having Sugar join us at the clinic at first and we would forget that she was there, and lock her inside. Around twilight or even after dark, sometimes a Murle would be passing the clinic and hear Sugar barking. They would hurry to tell us we had left our "maa" in the clinic. When we got there to let her out, we discovered she had climbed up on my examining table, pushed off all my equipment, and was lying there on the table like a lady of leisure. We felt it was her way of protesting because we had locked her in the clinic. She taught us to always remember her. Even your pets can teach you.

A MISSIONARY DOCTOR'S SIN

As the days progressively got hotter and the patient load also continued to increase, a real problem developed in my own life. As I have stated before, two days a week I went over to the government clinic in Pibor town. At that clinic, I expected to see the teachers, police, soldiers and other government workers. But as the days progressed, more and more of those people started coming to the afternoon clinics on our side of the river.

Now the Murle people would start gathering for the clinic around noon, although we wouldn't begin seeing people until 1 o'clock. We had someone stationed at the clinic to give out numbers to the people as they arrived, so we would be fair in seeing them in order of their arrival. The townspeople wouldn't get there until 1 o'clock or after, and they expected to be seen quickly because they had jobs, etc., in Pibor town.

Now, my Murle language ability was improving day by day, so by that time I was able to deliver a short understandable Bible message before we began the clinic, and explained to the Murle why we were there. I would tell them how much the Lord loved them and how He had made a way for them to become His children through the sacrificial death of Jesus. So, every day I would begin the clinic like that and always end it in prayer. I prayed the Lord would use His word in their hearts to open their spiritual eyes and ears. Yet after this spiritual ministry, these townspeople increasingly came and begged to be seen early.

I began to develop anger in my heart toward them and resented them trying to push ahead of the Murle who had been given numbers as they arrived. At first, I mildly scolded them about coming late and then wanting to be seen before the Murle. Because they had jobs, they argued that they should be seen before the Murle tribesmen, who had no such responsibilities. After scolding them, I would see them and give them their treatment. As this happened more and more frequently, I developed a much harsher attitude toward them and found myself haranguing them with longer and longer tirades

So, the clinics would start with me telling the patients that God had sent us there because He loved them and wanted to show His love to them through us. Then as the clinic began, because of my angry words with the townspeople, I negated everything I had said in the beginning devotional. I knew this was very unacceptable behavior for a child of God, so I went around most of the time with a terrible guilt complex because of this inexcusable anger.

Late one afternoon after having one of these tirades, on our way home Ginny said, "You know honey, I think you have a 'stronghold of anger.'"

I was startled at first to hear this, but as I thought about it, I realized she was right. There was no other explanation for my behavior, which was totally opposite of all that Jesus had taught us concerning the peace and joy to be seen in the lives of His followers. It was also totally opposite to the kind of behavior I wanted to live before the Murle as well as the townspeople.

Before going to bed that night, I had to repent and confess my sin to the Lord and claim the pulling down of the stronghold of anger. I used the weapon of warfare the Lord had made available to us as believers, found in **2 Corinthians 10:3-5**. Some may argue that we Christians, and especially missionaries, cannot develop "strongholds," but when we get rebellious, as I was at that time, I'm convinced it can easily happen.

How was I rebellious? The Lord had been convicting me that this anger was hurting my testimony before the Murle at the clinic and also the townspeople, but I had let the issue smolder without truly facing the truth. Basically, I had refused to repent and confess my sin. In fact, I justified it because I was blaming my actions on the behavior of the townspeople. So, what started as a little anger built up to be almost uncontrollable. I had allowed it to become a "stronghold" in my own life.

I do know this. After I confessed and got my heart right with the Lord, miracles began to happen. It seemed the attitude of the people completely changed and they stopped being so demanding. Also, I realized the Murles had all the time in the world and these townspeople really did have responsibilities. So, after that when they asked to be seen early, I politely asked the Murle next in line if it was all right with them for me to see the person from town before them. They always said it was okay. The clinics took on a whole different atmosphere. I could sincerely preach to the Murle before starting and tell them God had provided a way for them to become His children through His Son, Jesus. I could honestly tell them God could bring peace into the hearts of those who trusted Him, because He had worked a miracle of peace in my own heart. **Eternal Fruit.**

ANOTHER LESSON: TWO GUYS ON AN AIRPLANE

Shortly after the above episode, the Lord taught me another tough lesson. It is wonderful that He never gives up on us and continually teaches us through many varied circumstances. This one started one day while I was at the government clinic. I had been steadily seeing patients for a couple of hours, when I heard an airplane overhead. Now, every day, early in the morning, we talked by radio to our ACROSS headquarters in Juba and they would tell us if they were sending an airplane to Pibor that day. They had said nothing that morning about an airplane coming. I was puzzled as to why an airplane was landing at Pibor, but after looking out the door, I saw it was not our airplane. It was a different plane. I didn't think about it again.

Just as I was finishing my last couple of patients, a policeman came to the clinic door to announce there were two men on that airplane who wanted to speak to me. I couldn't imagine who they might be or what they wanted with me. I finished seeing my last patient and then set out to find them, to see what they wanted. They weren't at the local administrator's office or at the police station, but after a while, I found them at the school.

Now, there is quite a story about this school building where I found these men. Just before the beginning of the first civil war in Sudan, back in the 1950s, the US government had a program to help in the development of Southern

Sudan. It was a very ambitious project, but they had sent a crew and building supplies to build a school at Pibor Post. The builders had made many cement blocks and had put up steel frames for several buildings, but before they could start the actual building program, the war started in earnest and they were evacuated. All the building materials had been scattered here and there during the twenty-plus years before it was safe for expatriates to again come to Pibor.

Some of the first folks to come back were ACROSS personnel in the late 1970s. One of these was a diligent and hard-working man who decided he could help with this school project. He stayed at Pibor several months and collected all the cement blocks he could find. They had been scattered all over the countryside, but he was able to complete a rather nice building that was now being used as a dormitory for rural boys to live in while they studied at the school.

The original classroom buildings were still useable but crowded. The rest of the steel frames brought to Pibor by US-AID were still standing without walls. ACROSS was proud of all the hard work their worker had done to get this dorm building completed and useable.

So, it was in this dorm building where I found the two mysterious guys from the airplane. It turned out there was no mystery. These were two men from the Government of Southern Sudan in Juba. At that time, the government was semi-autonomous, and these men had come on a fact-finding trip to see about conditions at Pibor Post. One of the men was from the Ministry of Health and the other was from the Ministry of Education. So, we all introduced ourselves and everything was cordial for about two minutes.

After those two minutes, things went downhill for the rest of our time together. First, they told me what a terrible job I was doing as a doctor at Pibor. Then they told me what a poor job ACROSS had done in helping out at the school. I couldn't believe my ears. To be honest, I sort of felt that I was a hero to even come as a doctor to Pibor. I had heard that the Ministry of Health couldn't even get a Sudanese nurse to come to Pibor because conditions were so poor.

Then for them to say that ACROSS had done a poor job with the school project was unbelievable. It was almost a miracle that enough building materials had been collected after twenty years to put even one building together. Yet there it was, and we were meeting in it. Totally unprepared for such a meeting, I had to stand there and listen to them for about forty minutes. After they dismissed me, they got on their airplane and flew away

I was devastated and heartsick. In my depression, I plodded the two miles or so to our house to give Ginny the "good" news.

"I don't even know why we are here," I told her when I got home.

It seemed my world was crashing down around me. After all we had done to come and bring a witness to the Murle, it seemed none of it was appreciated. I numbly went through my clinic work that afternoon but with a heavy heart.

For the next two or three weeks, I stayed depressed, and even though I prayed a lot and read my Bible every day, I had no joy and there seemed to be a dark cloud over me all the time. I remember a character named Mr. Btfsplk in the comic strip *Lil Abner*, who had a dark rain cloud that followed him and rained on him all the time. He was always sad and depressed about everything. Well, I felt like Mr. Btfsplk.

And then, one morning as I was praying and lamenting to God about my bad fortune and feeling sorry for myself, He seemed to speak to my heart.

He said, "Last year when you heard that message about 'servanthood,' you asked Me to teach you how to be a servant and now, I sent two guys on an airplane to give you that lesson, but you have become all upset about it."

Then it all became clear to me. In Jesus' parable about the servant **(Luke 17:7-10),** He stressed we are only supposed to do as our Master bids us and not to expect to be thanked for what we do. He seemed to point out that I was not called to Pibor by the Ministry of Health or the Ministry of Education, but God was the one who called me there and He was the only one who needed to be pleased with my ministry. I confessed my sin of complaining and asked Him to forgive me. Our Lord is so good. In a few moments, He took away the cloud of depression and restored my joy (actually it was His joy) in my heart. I did learn a lot about how to be His servant in the process.

These were exciting lessons, but would you believe? There were to be even more exciting lessons to learn in the months that followed. However, we will come back to them as our story unfolds in the chapters ahead.

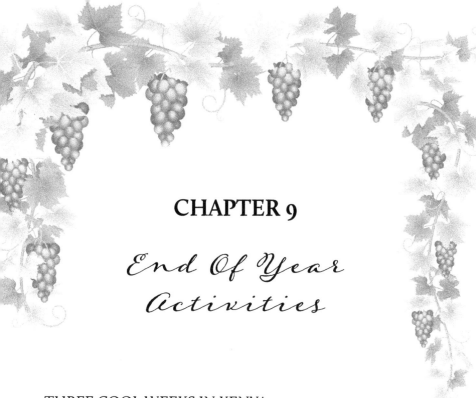

CHAPTER 9

End Of Year Activities

THREE COOL WEEKS IN KENYA

We had arrived at Pibor Post early in April of 1980, and by October, it seemed we had been there forever. ACROSS had a policy that their personnel were to leave their stations for some rest and recreation after six months of duty, so we took our three weeks leave around the middle of October and traveled to Kenya. It was so good to see Cathy at her school and spend some time with her, mainly on the weekends.

The second week, during the days when she was in school, we went to a mountain cabin in the highlands near her school. AIM (Africa Inland Mission) made it available for rent to folks from all the other mission organizations. Fortunately, for the week we needed it there were no requests, so we were able to stay the entire week. We took our cassette player with many Bible study cassettes and inspirational messages to listen to.

God blessed us spiritually during those days, plus the cool atmosphere was such a blessing after leaving hot Pibor.

On the weekends, we had good fellowship with Cathy, a junior now in high school, and her friends. The AIM mission also had a guest house in the same compound as RVA, so it was very convenient for the parents of boarding students to book in and be close to their children during their visits. Almost every weekend there were soccer, rugby or basketball games and we always enjoyed going to them with Cathy to cheer for RVA. These activities were a wonderful change from life at Pibor.

The last week of our leave we spent in Nairobi shopping for ourselves, the Bodenhamers and Haspels, since there were no shops at Pibor that sold anything. We bought canned goods of vegetables, meats, and soups to last for the next several months. However, because airplanes were small, we had to limit the weight of our purchases to the amount that could be put in the plane. Also, if there were some priority items needed for mission projects, then personal items were left to arrive on the next flight into Pibor. Since the plane came almost every two weeks, that was no problem.

When our three weeks were up, we flew back to Pibor, arriving on November 7, 1980. Usually this was the hottest time of the year with no cooling rains, but because of the Lord's special blessings that year we had some good rains in November and December. You remember we told you earlier how God blessed the Murle by giving them an extra crop of millet. God knew their needs, and He blessed us too, rounding out the sixteen inches we had prayed for.

That truly was a big miracle.

We can never comprehend what a wonderful and all-powerful Lord we have. So, we came back from our cool stay in the Kenya highlands, and immediately saw the Lord's miracle of rain. And actually, we were able to enjoy cooler days in the midst of the hot season at Pibor. The Murle told us the year before in late November, the river was only ankle deep, but this year the river was full even in November.

A WELCOME VISITOR

Our first visitor to come and welcome us back was our friend Nyati, who had miraculously been saved from the terrible shoulder and chest wound. When we left for Kenya, he was very much improved physically but was still very depressed, mentally and emotionally, because of his paralyzed left arm and the shock of the whole episode. During the days before our departure, we found it difficult to even coax him to walk 100 feet from his room in the hospital to the clinic for his dressing changes. However, on our return from Kenya, he voluntarily walked over 100 yards to our house with seemingly little effort and was smiling and greeted us warmly. His huge wound was almost completely healed. God's miracles were being seen on every hand – in the weather, in physical healing, but also in Nyati's emotional and spiritual healing.

A GREAT IDEA

While we were in Kenya, we met our dear friends, Zeb and Evelyn Moss, who were working with the Baptist Media Department in Nairobi. They were in the process of recording lots of gospel and music cassettes for different unevangelized tribes in East Africa, like the Murle. As they told us about their work, we realized they needed to come to Pibor to record some of the Pibor music. So, we invited them to come.

We had no idea where we would find the funds for their visit, but God already had that problem solved. In fact, when Zeb looked at his budget, he found that funds were already there. Zeb had been given some funds in his budget for work in new areas and the Pibor project certainly was a "new area." When we invited them, we expected them to possibly be able to come after six months or a year, but miraculously their schedule was clear during the last weeks of November that very year. They came on November 24, on the same plane with Cathy, who was coming home for the Thanksgiving and Christmas holidays.

Their seven-day stay at Pibor was very profitable, and during that week they were able to make several gospel cassettes of the Murle music, which was very indigenous. Also, they recorded some good Murle testimonies, plus some dramas that became very useful in the clinic and village ministry. The people loved these messages and dramas that they could understand so much easier than our still poor Murle.

For the rest of our time at Pibor, I continued to lead our devotional before each clinic in my halting Murle. While the patients were waiting to come into the clinic, one of our young Murle workers sat on the porch with the patients and played these cassettes. The people really enjoyed them. In **Ephesians 3:20 we read: "Now to him who is able to do immeasurably more than all we ask or imagine."** Our faith was so small, we would never have thought to even ask for such a blessing as these cassettes, much less to imagine that the Lord would send the Mosses all the way to Pibor to make them with funds He had already provided. He truly does **meet all our needs according to His riches in glory in Christ Jesus (Phil 4:19).**

CLINIC ATTENDANCE DOUBLES

A few days after we returned from Kenya, a group of kob came through our area, crossing the river in front of our house. The Murle assumed these were the first few antelope of the very large herd that usually crossed at this time of the year. For some reason, possibly the unseasonable rains, the other antelope did not continue to come. The Murle, thinking the migration had arrived, came from many areas in droves. So, because the kob did not come that month, they became the patients who came to our clinic, all afternoon and into the night. On examination, I found most of them had very superficial complaints. We believed the Lord had His own purpose in this. Of course, they were there waiting on the kob, but they were able to hear the gospel through the cassettes in a much better way than ever before.

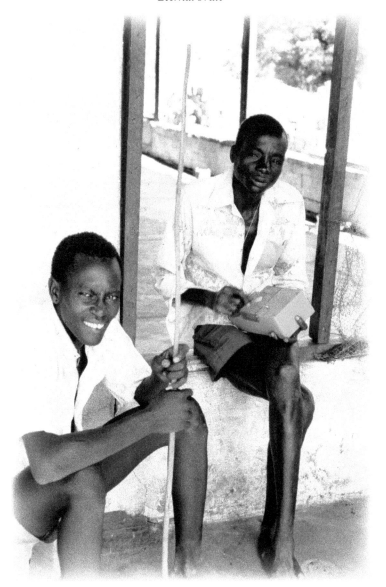

Patients listening to tapes by the clinic

During this time, we continued our minor surgery clinics, mainly entropion surgery of the eyelids and the removal of the keloid tumors of the skin. More and more people were coming for the entropion surgery, sometimes seven or eight a morning. We praised the Lord because He had given us this wonderful means to prevent much physical blindness but, in the process, He was allowing us to bring spiritual and eternal sight through our witness every day. This kind of response always encourages a medical person, because we knew people were being helped. They were encouraging their friends and neighbors to come for this simple eyelid surgery.

For two or three weeks the people waited on the kob to come and the clinic attendance was very heavy, but for some unknown reason the main part of the herd never did return to Pibor that year. Something caused them to change their normal migration route. After a while the Murle realized there would be no kob, so they made their way back to their villages. At that point our clinic attendance dropped to a more normal number.

ANOTHER SNAKEBITE CASE AND A NEW TREATMENT

After Cathy came home, she again was a great help in the clinic, especially with the surgeries, since Gwen had home schooling to do and Ginny was still teaching her literacy classes. One day they brought in a fresh snakebite case for me. I say "fresh" because most of the time the bites were too "old" or too toxic to treat with the method I will describe. In fact, most snakebites in Africa were beyond help from any type of treatment by the time they got to a doctor. The bites were usually on their arms or legs, requiring amputation.

When we first went to Pibor, I tried to keep snakebite anti-venom in case of such an emergency. It was very expensive and had a very short shelf-life, and expired before I had a chance to use it. I had a missionary doctor friend, Dr. Jack Tolar from Nigeria, who told me about a treatment an old doctor in San Antonio, Texas, had used successfully on rattlesnake bites before the development of effective anti-venom. I had already decided to try his method instead of wasting so much money on snakebite anti-venom I was never able to use.

Because they quickly brought in this young woman with a recent snakebite on her lower leg, I was able to give this treatment a good try. I explained to Cathy what I was going to do, since I had never tried this treatment before. After we had prayed for the Lord to be in control and give us His wisdom, I started to work. The venom had already caused some swelling. I knew without treatment, we would probably have to amputate her leg due to swelling and gangrene.

This new treatment consisted of putting a tourniquet several inches above the site of the bite, which prevented the venom from getting into the tissues and blood stream through the lymphatic circulation. Next, I took a liter of sterile saline solution and mixed a small amount of procaine local anesthetic with it and injected it under the skin all around the bite and then below and above the bite. With all that fluid, the leg swelled up like a balloon. After that I took a scalpel and began to cut hundreds of small slits in the skin all around the leg, above and below the bite. The procaine had done its work and she had no pain from all these incisions. I saw Cathy gritting her teeth as I was doing this.

Of course, the saline with the snake venom and a small amount of blood began to ooze out of the slits. After that, I took another liter of sterile saline solution, and with an IV tube and a needle flushed out all around the many slits in the skin, trying to get all the venom possible out of the tissues of her leg. After I had done all that, I put antibiotic ointment dressings on the leg and kept her overnight at the clinic.

SUCCESS

The next day when I took off the dressings, the swelling was down and there was no sign of infection in the leg. By the next day, the small slits had begun to heal and I was able to let the woman return home with some antibiotic ointment to apply to her leg. After a week when she returned, I checked her again. There was no other treatment necessary. It was so encouraging to see the Lord continuing to work miracles.

I had only had a casual conversation with Jack while we were having a break at a continuing medical education course in Kenya. I will never know why he told me about this snakebite treatment, but it had given me the idea of treating snakebites without anti-venom. God is in control of all things and can bring a miraculous healing out of a casual conversation.

Of course, since I had never seen such a treatment, Cathy was really wondering all during the procedure what the outcome would be. And you can believe that I was wondering about this too. The Lord taught us both that we can trust Him every minute of every day in all things. When we left Pibor there was a young woman walking on two good legs instead of having an amputation or having died of gangrene from post-snakebite infection.

CHRISTMAS AT PIBOR

We discovered that a Murle Christmas was very different than an American Christmas. After the Murle church service in the morning, they began to come to our home to visit. The early missionaries started this tradition and served tea to all the visitors. Since John Haspels worked directly with the church, many church people came to their side of the house, but of course, we helped with the entertaining there until about 4:30 in the afternoon. We had been witnessing to some of our neighbors, so they came to visit our side of the house even later. Christmas day turned out to be a long one for all of us, but one of many blessings.

Also, at that time we noticed the temperature was significantly lower in the mornings for several days, like 62-65 degrees. We learned later this was all the "winter" we would have at Pibor. Of course, it still warmed up to 95 degrees by afternoons. Christmas at Pibor was very different from what we had experienced in other countries, and even in America.

CHAPTER 10

God's Kingdom Work

ARE OUR EYES DECEIVING US?

One Sunday afternoon early in February 1981, we had a great shock. We heard a noise outside the house and when we looked out, we saw four white faces, three men and one woman, standing outside our fence. We did not recognize any of them and we weren't expecting company. We had not been notified on the radio by ACROSS either that any visitors were coming.

We hurried out to greet them by the fence where they were standing. They answered us in English, but not American English. We could tell English was not their first language, but we couldn't determine which country they were from. After we invited them in, they explained they were tourists. In our wildest dreams, we could never have imagined we would ever see a tourist coming to Pibor. As far as we were concerned, this place could easily be labeled the end of the world! Who in their right mind would come to Pibor as a tourist?

They explained there were eight of them who had come on this big German army surplus truck, and they were on their way to South Africa. They were German, Swiss and French. There were five men and three women on this safari. They had pooled their resources, had bought the truck in Germany, had it outfitted with chairs attached to the truck bed, and gotten as far as Pibor. They had camping equipment like tents, cooking utensils, camping stoves, large water containers, etc.

They had begun their trip in Germany, had driven down through Italy and then shipped the truck and themselves across the Mediterranean to Egypt, where they disembarked. Then they drove beside the Nile from Alexandra to Bor, where they had done what we did and cut across the plain until they arrived at Pibor. We wondered why in the world they would want to come to Pibor.

They explained. They had been reading some books about Sudan and seen pictures of some Sudanese women wearing huge lip plates in their bottom lips for beauty. They were planning to head east from Pibor to find that tribe so they could see these women with their own eyes and take some pictures of them. It turned out one of them worked for a Swiss news magazine and he was looking for a sensational story with pictures. We figured he planned to profit financially from this trip. The rest of them, however, seemed only to be on a lark. We learned later this kind of trip was a fad during those years for bored, affluent Europeans who wanted to get away from it all. It was true that at places like Pibor, you were really away from almost everything. At the end of their trip, they planned to sell the truck in South Africa and head back to Europe.

A COMMOM PRISON

As we fixed tea with some cookies we happened to have around for them, we exchanged stories. We, of course, felt we had nothing in common with these "tourists" from Europe, but we were wrong. The Swiss reporter told us he had been in Ethiopia in the days of the Communist rule. Naturally, our ears pricked up at that news because we must have been there at the same time. He went on to say the Communist government had arrested him and put him in prison in Addis Ababa. Since I had been arrested by that government and had been incarcerated for two weeks myself in Addis Ababa, I could understand the kind of stress he had experienced.

I asked him the date of his arrest and which prison he was held in. Would you believe? He had been locked up in the same prison I had been in. What kind of odds are there for two people to meet at Pibor Post, Sudan, one an American and the other a European, who were both locked up in the same Ethiopian prison in 1977?

As a result, he became very interested in me and what I was doing there at Pibor. So, for the next couple of days, he followed me around to my clinics—the one in town and the one at the old hospital. He watched me as I saw patients, photographing me as I worked, and even took pictures of all our mission work. Since none of these visitors were evangelical Christians, they really couldn't understand why we were there or even why we were helping the Murle with our medical work and our teaching. This gave us a wonderful opportunity to share with them what the Lord had done in our hearts and then how He had led us to come to Pibor.

We heard from this man several times after he left our area. In the next months he sent us some clippings from his news magazine. He had written some articles about Pibor, even illustrating them with pictures of our houses and clinics. His articles also told about our work there at Pibor among the Murle.

MOVED ON TO SEE THE LIP PLATE LADIES

Our visitors stayed in the Pibor area for a few more days, but one day came by to inform us they were moving on that day. They were heading east to see "the ladies with the big flapping lips," as they described them. They got directions from the local governor and the army commandant and headed east into unknown territory. They didn't know exactly where they were going, but they assured us their truck was manufactured according to impeccable German engineering standards and was almost impossible to break down or get stuck. Since most of the plains around Pibor had dried considerably by this time, we felt they were very unlikely to have any trouble. But both of us were very wrong.

THE VISITORS RETURNED

Three days after they roared off, waving to us as they passed our homes, we saw two of the men at our back fence again. They wanted us to help them because the impossible had happened. They were stuck in the mud out on the plain. They told us they had dug with their shovels for the past two days and also had hired some Murle men who had come to watch what these white men were doing. These Murle men had helped them dig, but even with all the extra help they couldn't get the truck out.

They had walked back to our house since it was closer than town from where their truck was stuck, to ask us for help. We explained to them that none of our vehicles would be able to pull their big truck out of a mudhole, but we would gladly drive them over to town to the army camp. We knew the army did have a large four-wheel drive military truck that might be able to help them. When we got to the army camp, the commandant told us the truck was not there but was coming back from Bor with supplies in the next few days. He also said that if the "tourists" would help him with fuel, then they could have the use of the truck to help them get their truck out.

We were curious to see the place where they had gotten stuck, so we drove those two fellows out to the place where the others were waiting. They reported to their companions what the commandant had told them. We got out to look around and could hardly believe our eyes. The truck was definitely stuck, but probably in the **only** large mudhole between Pibor and the eastern border of Sudan. We figured they were so confident of the German engineering that they decided to drive through this huge mudhole, feeling sure they would not get stuck. They could have driven around it. In our past twenty-plus years of experience in Africa, I had come to the conclusion that African terrain many times had some innate power to overcome or block all of our technological advances in travel and communication. These folks had learned this lesson the hard way.

They were still digging when we arrived and some of the Murle men were still there helping them, but they looked very tired and discouraged. They were glad to hear help was on the way, but not too happy to hear it would be another few days before the army truck would arrive.

The few days they were in Pibor they had stayed in a government "guest house" the local administrator had available to house any government workers or technicians who might be sent to Pibor to work on requested projects. The amenities and furnishings at this "guest house" were very limited, almost nonexistent, except for a roof overhead and some very spartan beds. But probably it had been better than sleeping in their truck and living out of it.

HELP FROM THE ARMY

Fortunately, the travelers had brought along a good supply of extra fuel and would be able to help the commandant with some extra fuel for his military vehicle. Since they had planned to camp out all the way to South Africa, they also had large containers of water that would probably last a week with conservative use. They had filled these containers at the Pibor pump with the clean water from the deep well that we used ourselves during the dry season, when one of our tanks had been contaminated with bad leaves.

We took a couple of them back to Pibor so they would be there when the army truck arrived. They could also urge the commandant to send his drivers ASAP to help them get on their way. Fortunately, the commandant's time schedule was correct (which was not always the case in Africa) and the army vehicle did arrive after two days. The commandant kept his word and sent it to the site of their muddy debacle. With the cables the Europeans had with them, the army truck was able to pull their truck out of the mud very quickly.

We had gone with the army vehicle just to see what happened, because we didn't have interesting things like this happen very often at Pibor. Everyone cheered when the truck came out of the mudhole. As they were leaving, we realized the Murle weren't the only surprises at Pibor, nor were they the only people we were sent there to minister to.

We believed these Europeans did not come to Pibor "by chance" because God let us minister to them as well as the Murle. As these folks drove down the eastern side of the African continent in the next few months, they had our testimony about God's love for them, plus several Bibles we had given them. They would be able to read about God's love and we prayed they would read those Bibles. Also, we prayed that for the few days they were there around us, they had recognized the love of the Lord expressed through our lives as we ministered to the Murle. This is an example of how our Lord works in and through our lives and reminds us He is very much in control of circumstances too. He has ways to use us in His Kingdom's work that we can never fathom. He had just brought some people from another country for us to minister to as we shared about our work, and we were able to send them on their way with Bibles, God's Word.

OTHER WHITE FACES COME TO PIBOR

Shortly after the tourists left, some other white faces showed up at Pibor. Oil had been discovered north of us on the western side of the Nile, but the oil companies were sure there was oil in the Pibor area also. So, the Total Oil Company of France sent some geologists to Pibor to run some seismic tests to verify their theory of oil deposits underground. These men stayed for over a month with all their equipment, setting off small blasts here and there. They took readings concerning the possibility of oil in the area.

They weren't very talkative about their findings, but we got the impression there were substantial deposits of oil under Murle land.

The civil war erupted full blast within eighteen months, so no development of these reserves was ever undertaken. In fact, the war in Sudan is primarily about oil, although the two sides state the main cause is usually because of a clash of religion and culture. If it were not for the rich deposits of oil in Southern Sudan, the northern government would probably gladly let the south go on its own way.

As it is, the southern rebels also want the wealth that will come from the oil, and of course, the northern government is going to do all it can to keep the wealth under its jurisdiction. From all reports there is enough oil there to make the whole country rich, if they would come to the bargaining table and be willing to share. Greed is one of the most destructive weapons that Satan uses to destroy people and nations.

UNEXPECTED RESOURCES AT OUR DISPOSAL

Shortly after this, we received a notice from ACROSS HQ in Juba that we were expected to build some rural clinic building in the Pibor area. That was a surprise to us because no one had ever mentioned it to us before. A few days later, they also informed us that an ACROSS builder was coming to help with this building project. We were glad to hear that news, but we had not requested funds for any extra clinic buildings in our medical budget. My understanding was that I was to supervise the Pibor clinics on both the mission side and the town side. I had budgeted for medical equipment and also for medicine subsidies for treating all these patients, but I had not included any funds for any kind of buildings.

In case you are wondering where a builder and his family would live, I need to explain that by this time the Haspels had moved on to another place past Pibor, so their end of the house was vacant. The builder and his family would be our new housemates. When the builder, Jack Swart, arrived with his wife, Debbie and their two children, I told him our dilemma. We began to pray with them about it. Within a week or so, we got a message from ACROSS, telling us a Dutch doctor was flying in to Pibor to consult with me about the medical work in the whole Jonglei province.

When she arrived, I realized she had actually been appointed by the Southern Sudanese government to oversee the medical work in our whole area. The Dutch government had a large project in Bor, which included agricultural development as well as supervising the medical projects for the province. I shared with her about the recent surprise revelation that we were supposed to build some of the rural clinics and the fact that we had no funds in our budget for such buildings. Much to my surprise and delight, she assured me funds for the building were no problem. She said she had a very adequate budget that came through the government of the Netherlands and she would gladly share it with us if we would let our builder supervise the project.

Our God is so good. He can even call in the resources of foreign nations when needed. Of course, when Jack had come to Pibor and found that one of his projects was to build some buildings and there wasn't any money, he began to wonder if he would be able to stay and be a part of the Pibor team. He had wanted to help to minister to the Murle. In fact, Jack had lived at Pibor as a young boy because his parents had been missionaries there. We laughed at him because he kept wandering around saying, "I don't remember this being so big," or "This seemed farther away than it does now." I am sure, as a child, things did look different.

In the space of one-half hour, my dilemma about no funds and his prospect of having no ministry were all solved. Both of these solutions came through a European doctor with funds from the government of the Netherlands.

CHAPTER 11

The Blood Covenant

LEARNING

E arlier, we had told you about how the Lord taught us some tough lessons on anger and servanthood, but the Lord still had more exciting things to teach us. The next lesson was going to open our spiritual eyes, plus do a transforming work in the lives of the Murle Christians. Before we went to Sudan, while we were still in Kenya, going to our rural clinics every week, we traveled by car and listened to many sermon and Bible study cassettes in the course of our travels. We heard an illustration about a great missionary to Africa who was having a very difficult time reaching a certain tribe.

Since it has been over twenty years since I heard it, I'm sure some of the details may be fuzzy, but I'll share it as I remember it. This missionary was preaching his heart out to a certain tribe but was having very few results. The people seemed to have no interest in listening when he spoke to them. He tried to explain to them that he had wonderful news that could transform their lives, but they showed little inclination to listen. He lamented about this to his trusted African servant who went along with him to help carry his things from village to village.

One day his servant said to him, "If you really want these people to listen to you, you need to cut a covenant with the paramount chief."

The missionary had never heard about a covenant but was willing to learn. So, he asked the servant to explain to him what cutting a covenant meant. He did explain it and then the missionary asked him if he thought he could arrange this with the chief. The missionary understood that doing this meant he would become a "blood covenant" brother with the chief.

To his surprise, the chief agreed, and set a day for the cutting of the covenant. Then the servant added something that shocked the missionary. He said that it was customary for them to exchange gifts at the ceremony. He added that the chief had decided the missionary needed to give him the nanny goat he took with him everywhere. This nanny goat was important to the missionary because it supplied milk the doctors had prescribed for his chronic stomach problem. But there was more. The chief would then give the missionary a very special spear he was having prepared.

The missionary was annoyed that the chief, who had many goats, would ask for his only goat and fumed that a spear was the last thing in the world he needed. The servant urged him to do as the chief asked, despite the irrationality of the chief's demand. It was much like the servants of Naaman, in the Old Testament, who urged him to obey Elijah's orders about washing in the Jordan to cure his leprosy **(2 Kings 5:9-14).** The servant assured the missionary that he could easily find him another goat. So, despite his misgivings, this doubting missionary kept his appointment and took the chief his nanny goat. They went through the covenant ceremony and then exchanged the gifts. The chief's spear truly was a spectacular looking spear.

Anyway, as the story goes, every time this man of God went to a different village and they put up his tent, the servant would stick the spear in the ground in front of the tent. Then **all** the people would come and listen intently to what the missionary had to tell them concerning Jesus. The end result was that many became Christians in that tribe.

We had never thought about the "blood covenant" concept being a useful tool in our ministry in Africa. We weren't even sure people would understand it and we had never heard a word for covenant in any language we had studied. So, we just forgot about it. We got busy with the clinic work in Kenya and never did follow up on a study of the "blood covenant" belief and practices among the East African tribes we were working among in Kenya.

GOD HAS HIS OWN WAYS

God has His ways of getting our attention. Sometime late in our first year at Pibor, we received a tape series from one of our prayer partners. There were about six cassettes on the significance of the blood covenant in the Bible. By this time, we had almost forgotten about the message we had heard on the tape in Kenya, but we were glad to get these tapes to learn more about the blood covenant. This tape series did jog our memory about the significance of covenant relationships among African tribes. These tapes were very good and contained many facts about covenant that we had never learned in our Bible courses in college. Nor any of the courses I had studied at seminary during my one semester seminary career.

These tapes came during what we call the winter months here in the USA, but by that time we had learned there weren't any *winter* months in Sudan. Except maybe those three or four days with cool mornings before Christmas.

We listened to these tapes carefully, since the Lord had planted that seed of interest in our hearts back in Kenya before we came to Sudan. Again, we failed to follow up on them. I guess our excuse could have been that we were still learning the Murle language and we didn't know where or how to start teaching or even talking about covenants. I know I have said before how wonderful it is that the Lord doesn't give up on us, but is patient until we are willing to learn what He needs to teach us. So, a few months later we got **another set** of cassettes, by a different teacher, but on the same subject – "The Blood Covenant."

This time the tapes were sent by Dr. T.W. Hunt, one of our prayer partners. We knew he was a man of God whom God used to speak to many people, and now God was using him to speak to us. This time the Lord really got our attention. Some of us are very thick-headed. We diligently listened to these messages and then determined that we would discover what the Lord wanted us to teach the Murle about covenant. Actually, that thought was all wrong. We found out God wanted to teach **us** about covenant through the tapes, but also to teach us through the Murle, because they already knew lots about a covenant relationship.

A BREAKTHROUGH

So, for a couple of months during the dry season, we tried to find out from the Murle what they believed about the practice of cutting covenants. Our Murle language vocabulary was improving but still was inadequate. We had a hard time describing to them what a covenant was. We asked lots of people in every way we could think of concerning a covenant relationship developed between two Murle. Finally, one of the young men we asked came up with the idea that we should ask some of the older people, because he thought they might know more about such things than his generation.

That was our breakthrough, because we found out the older Murle people knew a lot about covenant and covenant relationships. Although the older people were the only ones who knew the details, when they described the practice to younger people, then the younger people began to understand. They recalled instances of how their families had been affected by covenants and covenant relationships.

We discovered the Murle had both positive and negative types of covenants. They talked more about the negative type covenant than the positive type covenant. Many of them could remember hearing of positive covenant relationships too, formed in the old days during the tribal wars. When the Murle warriors were fighting other tribes for cattle or grazing rights, sometimes one young man might rescue another during a battle and save his life. After the war, the family of the rescued one would decide they should "cut a covenant" with the family of the rescuer. They did that by calling the families together. Then they killed an animal, because blood was essential in making a covenant. After that they ate a meal together. From that time on, these two families were in a covenant relationship.

COVENANTS BETWEEN TRIBES

The older people we talked to even remembered a covenant being made between two tribes. They recalled that a family of the Anuak tribe had helped a family of the Murle tribe during a time of famine, and a covenant was cut between those two families. Again, nothing could sever that relationship, even though they were of different tribes, because they had "cut a covenant." The Anuak were an agricultural people and the Murle were a cattle people. They really were very different but could help each other, because in a covenant relationship they were totally committed to each other.

NEGATIVE COVENANTS

The most frequent type of covenant known by the generation of Murle we worked with was a negative covenant that didn't initially involve "cutting a covenant" or sacrificing an animal. This kind of covenant occurred when a dispute arose between two Murle and it became irreconcilable. Then one of the parties would say the words "Tet Zoch" and break a stick in front of everyone present. The words, "Tet Zoch," literally mean "cut the foot," but it seemed to have a great and lasting significance when spoken under these circumstances. After that there was never any relationship or communication between these two parties or families. In fact, only hostility existed between them. The most important fact we learned was that to the Murle, a covenant could never be broken – whether positive or negative. Covenants in the

Murle tradition are forever. However, they did admit that in the case of this negative covenant, where they only broke a stick, there was a possibility of reconciliation. If both parties decided they had made a terrible mistake and wanted to revoke the negative covenant, the way to do that did involve an animal sacrifice.

Now the Murle are a cattle people. Because of this, they have hundreds of names in their language for every color and combination of colors for their cattle. Every Murle male, during puberty, is given a special calf from the family herd. Many times, he is even given the name of his special animal, and he is known by that name the rest of his life. This animal becomes beloved in this young boy's eyes and they are special friends for life.

To revoke the negative covenant, the one who wanted to break the covenant has to bring his special animal (which took much soul searching, because he loved that cow) before both families. Because the shedding of blood is important in a covenant relationship, the special animal is sacrificed. A covenant meal is eaten and then the negative covenant is totally revoked and the two parties are reconciled. This reconciliation is just as binding as the separation caused by the original words, "Tet Zoch."

As we taught them the Bible, this explained perfectly what happened when people received Jesus as their personal Savior. Because Jesus became the blood sacrifice between a person and God, when a person became a believer, he or she entered into a covenant relationship with God. Because of Adam's sin in the book of Genesis, everyone born after him was separated from God and needed God's forgiveness. God didn't sacrifice an animal, but sent His only Son as a sacrifice, and by Jesus' death and shed blood, God made a way for anyone who received Jesus as their Savior to become reconciled to Him in a covenant relationship. Understanding this about covenants made a tremendous difference in the Murles' walk with the Lord. They knew it was an everlasting decision and binding for life. No one took the step of becoming a Christian after that unless they were totally committed to their walk with the Lord for life.

However, when our believers realized that eating blood was forbidden by God beginning with Noah **(Gen. 9:4)** and continuing through the Mosaic covenant (**Lev. 17:11, 12**) and even in the New Testament (**Acts 15:29**), they decided even if they starved, they would not drink blood again. We didn't feel we should make such a decision for them, since this was a long-standing practice in their culture and probably had been useful in saving lives during the times of severe hunger. So, when they asked us, we just pointed these scriptures to them and told them to pray about the matter. Some of them agreed with this and others did not. We left Pibor while this discussion was going on, so we did not know how it was resolved. What do you think?

After we learned about their covenant practices, we asked them what would happen if someone broke a covenant – either positive or negative. They were astounded that we would even ask such a thing.

They said, "**Nobody** would ever break a covenant!"

We couldn't believe this and told them people in the USA were always signing contracts and making binding agreements, but many times they broke them. They said that would never happen in a Murle covenant relationship. We kept insisting that surely some Murle would break a covenant some time or other, so what would happen?

They said, "It would almost never happen, but **if** a Murle breaks a covenant, he will die."

Then they went on to say they had known of people who had broken a covenant – and they died. Nobody poisoned them, nobody killed them, they just died. They knew that was what happened to people who broke covenants. It is amazing how we, in our sophistication, think cultures like ours are so very superior to ones like theirs. They are way ahead of us in their commitment in keeping covenants and some of their standards are much higher than our lukewarm Western standards.

TOBACCO AND FETISHES

I told you how most of the Murle smoked tobacco. Because of their hunger periods during the dry season, it was just part of their lifestyle. It helped to alleviate hunger pangs. However, as addicted as they were to it, when they understood they were in a blood covenant relationship with God through the blood of His Son and that their bodies were the temple of the Holy Spirit, they brought their tobacco to church and burned all of it in front of everyone who was there. They said that now because they understood their bodies were the temple of the Holy Spirit, they didn't want to pollute their bodies with tobacco. We, of course, had felt that the smoking of tobacco was detrimental to their health, but we had never mentioned that to them, so we knew these convictions were directly from the Holy Spirit.

Even though they were not as a tribe always living in constant fear of evil spirits, they did go to certain medicine women, especially for their children, who would give them fetishes or charms to provide good luck or bring healing. So, the next move on the part of the believers was to bring all their fetishes before the Lord and the congregation and burn them. Then they testified that they were not planning to trust in these people anymore because they had put their lives in God's hands. Now they only trusted Him and Him alone, to protect them and heal them.

They continued to come to the clinics, however, because they believed God does heal and had seen that He used medicine many times in His healing process. We did not enter into any of these discussions about the above things because we knew God would lead them. We didn't want them doing things this drastic because of anything we said to them.

A VERY DIFFICULT DECISION

One of the biggest social gatherings of the Murle tribe every year was the "Tribal Dances," which attracted Murle men and boys and women and girls from all over their territory. These dances were held after the harvest of their meager crops and before the severe part of the dry season. At that time, they had to take their cattle to the cattle camps where there was still some grass and water.

These dances lasted for several days and there was much laughing and singing and clapping and jumping. The last one had been held right outside our compound under a very large tamarind tree that was also surrounded by other shade trees. It seemed to us the whole tribe came, so there were hundreds of people (maybe more) coming and going during the whole celebration. Also, there was lots of noise only during the day, thank goodness.

We didn't attend but watched just outside our gate that year, enjoying the festivities. Because the believers had learned and understood about covenant, the Lord convicted them about holiness. They came to tell us they could not take part in the "Tribal Dances" again. We knew this event was the highlight of the whole year for everyone in the Murle tribe, so we couldn't understand why they felt they must exclude themselves from it.

Then they explained to us why they had made this decision. They said during those dances, there were many illicit sexual practices going on. Certain men and women would signal each other during the dance and then later would have a secret, adulterous relationship. This included married men and women as well as young people. The Christians in our church had decided they would continue to gather with the people for the festivities, but they could no longer take part in the dances themselves. We knew only the Spirit of the Lord could have convinced and convicted them to make this momentous decision.

The next year, we prayed that during the dances their testimony and their lives would be a witness to all the rest of the Murle. We praised the Lord for convicting them and claimed the Holy Spirit to continue His work through their lives. In the pages ahead, you will see He did that in a mighty way.

MARRIAGE

The Murle did not as yet have the concept that marriage was also a covenant relationship. We began to teach this truth and prayed in the ensuing years after we left there that marriage would become a holy covenant relationship with them. They had seen our marriage and the other missionaries' marriages, so perhaps they prayed about their marriages too. One of the women asked Ginny one day her opinion about a decision she had to make. It seems a nearby man wanted to use her house to have sex with a woman who was not his wife. She didn't feel it would be right but asked Ginny for advice. Ginny told her she was right and shouldn't let them use her house to do that. So, I knew they were thinking about marriage.

WE FINALLY UNDERSTOOD

We praise the Lord He didn't give up on us and kept teaching us about covenant despite our laziness. God knew the Murle understood about covenant. He just had to wait until we learned about it too. We Westerners have drifted so far away from the biblical concept of covenant, we would never have dreamed that the lives of so many Murle could be transformed in such a phenomenal way. It was just because they believe so ardently in the eternal nature of and irrevocability of a covenant relationship.

We are convinced if American Christians would ever understand they had entered into a covenant relationship with Almighty God through the blood of His Son Jesus when they received Him as their Lord and Savior, then their lives would be as exciting and obedient as the Murle. In a covenant relationship in ancient days, and in many tribes who still practice it in our day, when two people enter into a covenant relationship, all the resources of each is made available to the other. It stands to reason if one of those in the covenant with us is the Creator God of the universe, it is mindboggling to even try to comprehend what He is making available to us, and we don't even understand this. Just think what He could do in and through us. How we pray that all American Christians would understand what it means to be in a covenant relationship with God. We know it would truly be a transforming experience for them and for everyone around them.

CHAPTER 12

Plastic Surgeries And The BBC

BUSH DOCTOR TO PLASTIC SURGEON

Our second rainy season had begun and was also a good one. We had seen the Lord's miraculous provision for rain during the first year, so our prayer priority this second year was not rain. Therefore, we didn't keep as accurate a record during the second year as we did the first year.

Also, the Murle people gradually came to accept us and our way of life. They came to understand we truly loved them and were there to help them. This was especially true of Ginny's students, but also through the friends we had made from all my clinic work and surgeries.

The bulk of our first surgeries consisted mainly of the entropion repair cases for the correcting of the damage caused by the trachoma infection of the eyelids. This was the disease that turned the eyelashes under so they scraped on the eye itself when they blinked. Many were blind from trachoma. I also removed many keloid scars, which had been caused by infected tribal markings and ear piercing. There were also some very difficult obstetrical deliveries due to the large size of the fetus, which many times had died in the womb or the birth canal before the woman was brought to the clinic. These were usually very infected and very messy, but God was very good to me and I lost none of the mothers, even after the difficult destructive surgery required on the fetus to remove it.

FACIAL SURGERY

During the second year, we had a change in the most frequent type of surgery. It turned out to be plastic surgery. No, we did not do any liposuction or facelifts—the Murle would never conceive of such things. Besides that, they had no fat on their bodies to speak of that would require liposuction.

If you are wondering what I knew about plastic surgery, that definitely is a good question, because in general, I was clueless. Medical missionaries frequently find themselves doing things they have had little or no training for. However, this type of plastic surgery turned out to be very simple and even I could do it.

It started with some of Ginny's female students. In their culture nearly all Murle women had "cosmetic beauty aids" like a piece of bone or ivory inserted in a small opening in their lower lips and occasionally in their upper lips. How they performed these "operations" without anesthesia or sterile technique on teenage or younger girls, I will never understand. Nevertheless, somehow they did, with very primitive instruments. When the tradition started, I don't know, but it was almost universally in vogue by the time we arrived at Pibor.

However, two of the students came to Ginny and asked very quietly if she thought I could close that hole in their lower lip. Since they were around Ginny every day, they noticed she never had saliva or food running down her chin like they had. I'm sure they thought about it a long time, but finally decided these questionable "beauty aids" in their lips were more trouble than they were worth. So, Ginny came to me and asked if I could do this procedure. Since it could be done very simply and under local anesthesia, I agreed, thinking two or three such cases would not be a problem. However, word gets around fast in the African bush, and before long women were coming from everywhere in Murle-land, wanting me to close the holes in their bottom lips.

The number of entropion eyelid operations was declining because most of those in the tribe who needed them had come during our first year. So, the most frequent surgery in the clinic during our second year became this small plastic surgery procedure on the women's faces. I would do five to ten of them, two or three days a week on our surgical days. Like the entropion surgery, the demand for this little oper-ation was generated by news traveling from village to vil-lage by word of mouth. And the fact that they kept coming showed us the surgeries were obviously successful. Even though each case only took a few minutes, the large case-load used up a lot of time on our surgery days.

We were there to show the Lord's love to as many Murle as we could and to tell them about the great sacrifice our Lord Jesus made so that we, as sinners, could actually become His children. So, we thanked the Lord for allowing us to be at Pibor and prayed He would use all that we did to draw people to Himself. There was even a woman standing by our gate as we were leaving for furlough, calling out to get her lip repaired. We hollered back to her to wait until we returned. But unfortunately, we never went back.

After that period in my life, every time I heard somebody say, "Don't give me any of your lip" (a slang saying during my day), I would chuckle to myself, remembering all those Murle women who were willing to walk many miles to give a piece of their lips to me to close those troublesome holes. Because actually, all I did was cut out a small piece of tissue in the center of the hole, then put in a couple of sutures to close the skin. It was amazing how quickly they healed, and I don't remember many significant infections or deformities that developed afterward.

SUMMER WITH OUR CHILDREN

Since our boys were out of their universities for the summer, they again came to Pibor for their vacations. Some of you may ask how we "poor" missionaries could afford to fly our children all the way to Africa just for their vacation time. Actually, our mission board had a policy that furnished transportation one time for missionary kids (MK's) in college so they could be with their parents when they were separated due to their schooling. Our boys had used this way to come to Pibor the first summer, but this second summer was at our expense.

Many years before, we had decided that on the mission field and especially at places like Pibor where communication was so difficult, we would save our money for transportation for our kids to fly out to see us. Also, telephone calls (when we could get to a telephone) were also part of this money we saved. We did this the entire time we were on the mission field.

First Stan came in mid-May of 1981and then Mike came at the end of the month. Cathy's school wouldn't be out for vacation until July, but all three were able to overlap for a few weeks. The mission board always paid for transportation for boarding students, so Cathy's transportation was automatically covered. We had priority time to catch up on the lives of each one of them during that summer. This year was so much better because we did not have to deal with all the shooting of the year before while they were home. We did not have to dodge any bullets at any time while they were there.

Front: Mike, Cathy, and Stan. Back row: Ginny and Sam. Celebrating Mike's birthday

THE BBC AT PIBOR?

One day on our daily radio call with Juba, we had some exciting news. ACROSS sent word that a BBC team from England was coming to make a documentary film about the kob migration and the relationship the Murle tribe had with this annual movement of animals. It had long been well known in Kenya and Tanzania about the wildebeest migration and the effect it had on the Maasai and other tribes. No research or documentation had been done on the kob and the Murle tribe. This migration was not as large as that of the wildebeest, but the synergistic relationship with the Murle tribe would be interesting to people around the world, since it was in such an isolated part of Sudan and even Africa. Also, this migration had not received any publicity in the international press, compared to the larger migrations to the south.

So, some BBC programmers flew into Pibor to check out what was there and what would be needed to bring in their crew and equipment. Of course, they were delighted to find some Americans in the area and to learn that during the migration, the animals actually came through the area where we lived. With the extra space in the old hospital building, there was room for them to store their fuel and equipment. So, they arranged to send a large plane with several drums of diesel fuel for their helicopter and we promised them we would help move it to the old hospital for storage.

Since the river was full at that time, we hired some Murle men to roll the drums from the airstrip to the river. Then we had them rolled into the water, tied them together to make a raft, tied the raft to the back of the boat, and very slowly towed it up the river to the landing by the hospital. Because diesel fuel is lighter than water, these drums all floated and thus could be towed. Stopping in the river near the hospital building, we untied the drums from the boat and began to roll them up the riverbank toward the hospital, where we were to store them.

As we rolled them up one, of those unexpected African events occurred. No one could have anticipated it.

THE BEES

There was a hive of bees in one of the large trees nearby, and I guess they felt threatened by our approach because suddenly they attacked us. We all fled back to the river and jumped in. It so happened one of the BBC men turned out to be very allergic to bee stings. I knew this could be a very dangerous condition, even life-threatening. Fortunately, I had some adrenalin injections and steroid injections (another God thing), which I immediately gave him when the bees returned to their home. Even then. with the readily available medication, he had a difficult time that first night. Gradually, however, his reaction subsided and by the next evening, he was much better. He kept a good distance from that tree and those bees for the rest of his stay at Pibor. But we did get all the drums of fuel into the storage rooms and it was available for the rest of their project.

JOHN KAJAC AND THESE BEES

Word travels fast in Africa, even without telephones. John Kajac, a lad there in our church, heard about what had happened and decided he wanted some of that honey. So, he climbed up the tree to get it, but he lost his hold on a limb somehow and fell to the ground. He had a badly broken hip, which I couldn't repair at Pibor. We called the airplane and sent him to Kenya to find doctors who could operate on him and make it possible for him to walk again. He had never been away from Pibor and I'm sure he was terrified. First an airplane ride, customs, hospital, doctors he didn't know, and surgery. The doctors there were able to fix his hip. He walks straight and he knows all that happened to him was a miracle.

John Kajac He is the younger brother of Ngatiin, who had the bowel obstruction mentioned earlier. God is good. (Now, back to the BBC.)

The BBC crew was very friendly, and they truly did bring some very fancy equipment. One of the pieces was a microphone about a foot long, able to pick up sounds from a great distance with clarity. Plus, they also had some high-powered recorders that could be attached to the microphone. Now, our son, Stan, was a great bird watcher and had been trying to teach us about all the bird calls that were around us every day. Pibor really did have a great variety of African birds, and since we lived on the river, many of them were around us all the time.

So, Stan very boldly asked the supervisor (who happened to be the one with the bee sting allergy) if he could use the microphone and recorder until the crew came back in the fall to start the documentary film production. Since we had helped them so much with the fuel and medical assistance, he graciously let Stan use his equipment until they returned for the beginning of the kob migration. Stan had a great time recording all the bird calls for several weeks with all that fancy BBC equipment. Because the recordings were crystal clear, he was able to teach us about the different kinds of birds and their calls. After we left Pibor, from time to time we still listened to those recordings.

Stan, who made the recordings in 1981, died in Ethiopia in 1989 while doing volunteer water development work. He had completed his master's degree at Baylor University in 1988 in hydrogeology and went to Ethiopia as a volunteer in the summer of that year. While we were serving in Zanzibar (an island off the coast of Tanzania), on March 17, 1989, his truck accidentally fell over a cliff in Ethiopia as he was backing up to get back on to the road after taking pictures of the beautiful landscape. As his truck rolled down a steep canyon, he was thrown out and died instantly. Jerry Bedsole, our missionary friend and co-worker while we served in Ethiopia, called to give us the news of Stan's death. We were totally devastated, and made plans immediately to travel to Ethiopia. We chose to have his funeral there. We knew he would want to be buried there more than any other place in the world because he had grown up there and loved Ethiopia.

Sorry that I digressed from our Pibor story, but those Pibor bird recordings have been with us for many years and we still have them to remember Stan's hard work in trying to teach us the many beautiful bird sounds all around us on the river at Pibor. Our Lord is wonderful. He let all that fancy equipment of microphones and recorders come at that time, so in the years to come, we would have the tapes Stan made for us at Pibor. We call it an **Eternal Blessing**.

VISITS COME TO AN END

All good things always have to come to an end. Cathy had come for her month at home during August, and after a couple of weeks overlapping with her brothers, they had to leave to get back to their colleges. This second year their departure wasn't as stressful as the first year when they had to leave us with a small war going on around us. But it is always a sad day when we have to say good-bye to our children.

By this time, Cathy was becoming a very great help on the surgery days and also was becoming a very good cook. So, Ginny was relieved of much of her own stress during that month Cathy was home to help. Nevertheless, at the end of August she too had to leave to begin her last year at RVA. Normally we would have been very lonely when all the kids left us, but God had some exciting new experiences for us. We were going to get a vision of what it would mean for a tribe to have the completed New Testament in their own language for the first time.

A NEW TESTAMENT TRANSLATION

Toward the end of our second rainy season, the Arensens returned to Pibor and the translation of the Murle New Testament began in earnest. Of course, the Arensens had to settle into their home again after a year's absence, but when they were settled, Jon went straight to work. For about four years before their furlough to the USA, Jon had studied the Murle language and developed a good vocabulary and a conjugation of the verbs, etc. So, he was ready to start the translation.

Before that could happen, in a new language that had never been written, many decisions had to be made concerning orthography. That is the spelling of the sounds of the new language. There were some new sounds we do not have in English. To make the language easier to read, Jon chose to add some vowels and consonants to their alphabet to cover these different sounds. I won't go into detail, but it was exciting to see a language that had never been written being developed on paper right in front of our eyes.

John Atiel, a Murle teacher from Pibor with a fair knowledge of English, was Jon's helper. They worked daily on the translation in Jon's small office, which he had built out of poles and mud with a thatched roof, right in front of his own house. It even overlooked the river. This became his translation center and office. He had put large windows in the hut with screen over the openings so there would be a good circulation of air when any breeze was stirring in that hot Pibor climate.

We felt very privileged because Jon would invite us to come to his translation hut several times each week. He would spend a couple hours with us and report on his progress. He would toss out his ideas about the translation or orthography and get our opinions (for what they were worth). He even let us take some of the work they had done to test with our friends out in the village. That made us feel like we had a small part in this very important work. We didn't know at that time that in a couple of years we would actually be on the Murle New Testament translation team.

Before starting the translation, however, Jon decided to do a trial run on some other biblical texts. I think they started with the book of Jonah and then a few of the first chapters of Genesis. That way the Murle would have the creation story as background material. This turned out to be very helpful in deciding about some of the vocabulary words in the New Testament translation. Later, they finished the entire book of Genesis to publish it along with the New Testament, so the Murle Christians who had very little Bible knowledge would have this important book as background material when studying the New Testament.

THE BBC AND THE KOB RETURN

The fall portion of the kob migration usually started early in November, but it was past the middle of the month before the first animals came to our area that year. However, the BBC had scouted them with a helicopter and were there when the first animals started crossing the river in front of our house. I'm sure the crew had had many opportunities to photograph some of the herds before they got to Pibor, but at Pibor they were able to get pictures of how the Murle hunted them with their spears. At one time we counted up to fifteen animals being skinned and butchered on both sides of the river near our house. The BBC crew was right in the middle of the action. Jack Swart, the young ACROSS builder who was living in the Haspels' side of our house, got himself a spear and was able to bag a couple of kob in the river along with the Murle hunters. The Murle, the BBC, and the missionaries all got in on the "act."

The kob came through for about a week and there was much excitement among the Murle, and, we must admit, among the missionaries too. Our two boys took part in the hunt when the herd came through in May, the two years when they were with us, but they were already back at school during this November crossing. So, they missed the BBC filming of the migration.

CATHY'S TENT

After all the excitement of the kob and the BBC filming, life got back to what we might call "normal." We really weren't sure that life at Pibor could ever be described as normal. But since the rains had subsided, it became hotter by the day. Cathy came back to Pibor in December and was sleeping in a room we had partitioned between the two ends of our house. Her room was right in front of the kitchen for the other end of the house. Because it faced the river and there were a lot of trees and bushes outside, she never got even a slight breeze.

So, she had the brilliant idea of putting up our camping tent in the front yard and let it become her bedroom. Since there had been lions around during the rainy season, we were a bit apprehensive about her sleeping by herself out in the tent. She calmed our fears by assuring us that her dog,

Sugar, would be with her and would warn us of any danger. We let her carry out her plan and she slept in the tent all of her December vacation before she went back to school in January. She was happy to be out there with her dog.

Cathy's bedroom and one of Stan's bird houses

Also, Cathy was a welcome addition to our medical team, because after the excitement of the kob migration settled down, many Murle returned again for the "lip-plug" surgery. We realized it had become very popular among the women. Also a few of the entropion eyelid surgeries would wander in from time to time on surgery day. Ginny helped me with these surgeries when Cathy was at school, but when she was on vacation Ginny said the surgical clinics were Cathy's job.

A HORN ON THE CHEST

We did see some unusual cases. One that Cathy will always remember was a man with an infected wound on his chest. He gave a history of an injury several years before that had become infected, sometimes draining profusely, but other times it seemed to improve. However, it did not ever completely heal. When he came to us in December of 1982, there was a hard, bone-like projection about one inch in length attached to the center of the lesion, protruding from his chest wall. I had heard of such things, but in all my years in Africa, I had never seen one before. Cathy asked what this piece of bone was and I told her I thought it was called a "cutaneous horn," which is just what it looked like—a horn that forms in the skin. Usually they occur in cases of chronic skin lesions. The keratin layer of the skin, over several years, forms this horn. Actually cow's horns and other animal horns are formed just like this one.

The treatment is to excise the horn and treat the chronic infection that caused it. I excised it that day under local anesthesia and also tried to remove all the infected tissue in the area. That left a sizeable hole in his chest, but I filled it with antibiotics. Fortunately, the skin of his chest had good elasticity, and so with some undermining and stitches to bring the skin edges together, the end result turned out to be very nice.

So, the trend continued, and during those days, I couldn't seem to get away from plastic surgery. Because the Lord was good to me in my ignorance, I gave all the praise and glory to God for letting those good results of healing come from these surgeries. We saw many unusual cases, but when your surgery nurse is sleeping in a tent guarded by a Boxer dog, it should be expected that the cases would be unusual too.

CHAPTER 13

Sam's Disciple – Idris

A VERY HOT SPRINGTIME

As February passed into March, the weather continued to be very hot and dry. In one of our letters home in later March, we noted it had been 100 to 106 degrees in our living room for a whole week. And since we didn't expect any rains until May, these conditions were very discouraging. However, we knew the Lord said we would not be tested beyond what we could bear, so we trusted Him to send some rain or cooler weather in His perfect time.

Of course, in Sudan there is no such thing as springtime as we know it here in the USA. Just like there is no winter there, as we stated earlier. In fact, there are really only two seasons – rainy season and dry season. During the rainy season, the weather is much cooler, but after the rainy season the weather is basically hot most of the time. Occasionally during the dry season there was a cloudy day and\or a small shower that brought some welcome temporary relief during the normally scorching heat.

Cathy came home to Pibor for her spring vacation toward the end of March. As you may remember, this was done mainly for those students who were boarding from long distances. They had a whole month in April and August and December so they could spend some time with their families. Immediately she started helping with surgical cases and sometimes in the general clinic, but we didn't want to make her work too hard, since she needed some vacation time also.

The heat was very oppressive to her because she was coming from the cool Kenya highlands, where most evenings or early morning a sweater was needed. Enduring the heat, she pitched right in and helped with the surgical cases.

One of the first cases was a man who had been gored by a bull whose horn had pierced all the way through his upper arm. Fortunately, none of the major arteries were severed and the bone was not broken, but it took a lot of cleaning and scrubbing before we could put the skin back together on both sides of that arm. Fortunately, the Murle people in general had a very strong resistance to infections, and usually if we could get the wound clean, we were able to give minimal antibiotics, and the healing results were remarkable. That proved to be true in this case also.

THE MIRACLE THAT WAS IDRIS

Early in Jon and Barbara Arensen's experience at Pibor, they had befriended a young man name Idris. This young man was very intelligent and promising and had helped Jon in his early study of the Murle language. Jon and Barbara were impressed with his faithfulness in church attendance and felt he had great potential as a Christian leader. They decided to help him by sending him to Kenya to the Moffatt Bible College, an AIM (Africa Inland Mission) school. It was located near RVA, where Cathy went to boarding school.

Jon and Barbara had told us about Idris being in Kenya, and on our last R&R trip to Kenya, we had gone to Moffatt to find Idris, since it was so near where Cathy was in school. We did find him and introduced ourselves, since we had never met him. We were impressed with him too.

Jon had told us they hoped Idris would be a strong witness to the whole Murle tribe, and though he had only finished two years of his four-year course, they were praying he would come back to Pibor to live. They wanted him to carry on the evangelistic and discipling work we were doing until we returned the next year from our furlough. After Jon told us this possibility, we also began to pray that Idris would return to Pibor. We asked our prayer partners to pray also. I must be honest, Ginny and I didn't have much faith that he would actually return to Pibor before his four-year course was finished. It was such an honor for him to be able to study away from Pibor.

The Moffatt Bible College semester ended sometime late in March, and a few days after that, we could hardly believe our eyes when we saw Idris walking up to our house. He wanted to tell us he was planning to stay at least a year at Pibor. This was such a miracle that we could hardly believe it. However, God had been working in a mighty way in his life and he confessed that what had been interpreted by Jon and Barbara as Christian commitment was only a desire to learn.

However, during his first two years at Moffatt, he had become a true believer and it seems his return to Pibor was a result of this new, true relationship with the Lord. He also had a direct word from the Lord about this move, because he told us he had a dream, not once but three times, which he believed had to be from the Lord. In this dream he saw himself preaching in front of the people of his Murle tribe at Pibor. As far as we knew, he was the only Murle young man who had been given the opportunity to leave Sudan to study. And now he was willing to come back home with only half of his course completed to begin investing his life in the lives of his fellow Murle tribesmen. This was truly an awesome answer to prayer. **Eternal Fruit.**

MY DISCIPLE

Not only did he come ready to minister to his people as we had prayed, but he came to me and said, "Doctor, I want you to teach me all you can about what it means to follow Jesus." I had been praying since we came to Pibor for the opportunity to make disciples as Ginny had been able to do with her literacy and Bible classes. I was astounded and extremely thrilled.

By that time, we only had three more months left to work at Pibor before our time for furlough. I praised the Lord because He had brought "my" disciple to me all the way from Kenya. He had come with a ready heart (and a knowledge of English) and three months would be adequate, if we were diligent. Within a few days, we started meeting two or three hours a day on two afternoons a week, and truly I was able to pour my heart into Idris' heart. He had taken many courses and had studied the Bible, theology, and Church history, etc., but he had not been introduced to the concept of making disciples.

We had known the Lord had called us to minister to the Murle at Pibor, but now we saw very plainly He was continuing to work in the circumstances surrounding us. He had led Jon to Idris several years before and led him to sponsor Idris as a student at the Bible school even though it turned out that Idris wasn't a believer. Then God enlightened Idris and drew him to Himself. Then God put a hunger in his heart and began that molding process in him that Paul spoke of **in Romans 8:29 which says, "For those God foreknew he also predestined to be conformed to the likeness of his Son, that he might be the first born among many brothers."** Neither Idris nor I could have ever imagined what the cost was going to be for him to be molded into the image of God's Son. In the years to come, he would find out about that molding, which included much suffering but also much joy and many victories. But I have gotten ahead of our story.

So, Idris came to me with an eager heart that the Lord Himself had prepared and we started studying together God's priority about making disciples. We knew this was priority to God because this was the method Jesus chose when He introduced the Kingdom of God to the world. Also, it was the same method all the New Testament disciples used as they engaged in furthering the Kingdom.

How have we missed this salient fact from the life of Jesus and the ministry of His immediate disciples, and in turn their disciples? Somehow, in our day we have thought we could improve on Jesus' method by furthering the Kingdom of God by programs. As we read the New Testament, Jesus and His disciples brought in the Kingdom by developing disciples, who in turn developed other disciples, who in turn... etc., etc. This was all done by relationships and not programs. Paul put this process into words in **2 Timothy 2:2, "and the**

things you have heard me say in the presence of many witnesses, entrust to reliable men who will also be qualified to teach others." In fact, in that verse there are included five generations of believers. Barnabas was discipled by someone, then Paul was discipled by Barnabas, and then Paul discipled Timothy, and urged him to teach reliable men who would also be qualified to teach others. As I started teaching Idris, God actually started this process right there at Pibor. **Eternal Fruit.**

GOD'S MIRACLES CONTINUED

God is so good. And His timing is perfect. A few days after we started studying together, two young men came to Idris. They were new Christians and had become believers in a rather miraculous way. Again, God was working in His perfect timing.

A few months before in the dry season, these boys had been walking out on that long dry road between Pibor and Bor that I described in the first chapter. The details have left me as to why they were there, but they had no water or food, and after a few days, because they were so weak, they knew they were going to die. One of them knew some Christians at Pibor and said to the other one that he had heard these Christians pray. They had told him that God hears prayers, so he suggested they pray to God for water. They didn't know how to pray but just addressed God and asked Him to please save them and send some water. In a short time, a cloud appeared from nowhere, and when it got over them, it poured rain. Since they were lying on their backs, they opened their mouths, were refreshed, and continued on to Pibor.

So, since that time those two boys had become believers and had been wanting to know more and more about God who answered their prayer so wonderfully. I'm sure they talked to their Christian friends whom they had heard pray. These friends probably told them about Idris, who had gone to Kenya for study at a Bible school. When they heard that Idris had come back to Pibor, and was a Murle like them, they went to find him to ask him to teach them about God.   So, as I began to teach Idris, he then began to teach those two young men all the things I was teaching him. As he did this and they began to grow spiritually, he saw how wonderfully the concept of discipleship works. During the next weeks, the Lord blessed me as I poured all God's truth that I could into Idris, and He blessed Idris as he in turn poured God's truth into these two young men. As he was learning the concept of discipling, God had provided a means for him to see it actually worked in the lives of others. Since those days, Idris has been a true disciple and disciple maker. **Eternal Fruit.**

WEDDING AT PIBOR

Before we left Pibor for our furlough, Idris told us he had found a girl, Alawia, and he wanted to marry her. She was a Murle from a nearby village, so John Haspels married them. Not knowing the tradition of Murle weddings, we stepped in and offered to supply food and drinks after the wedding. We served several gallons of Kool-Aid and a large supply of cookies. I am sure no one had ever been to a wedding like that in Pibor — a preacher who performed the ceremony and food and drink from the missionaries' house. Oh well, it was a lot of fun and no one ever forgot it, I am: sure.

Sam and Idris after Idris' marriage

After that, instead of staying one year as he had planned, Idris stayed a couple of years at Pibor, preaching and teaching and discipling. Then he went back to Moffatt Bible College, but this time with a wife. He finished his course in the next two years.

During those two years Idris was away, the civil war in Sudan had heated up considerably, so instead of going back to Pibor, he went to Juba, the capital of Southern Sudan, and started a church there. Juba was the southernmost outpost of the northern Sudan Army, which was Moslem and very much opposed to Christianity. By that time, much of Southern Sudan was under control of rebel armies, but predominantly occupied by one of the larger groups, the Sudan People's Liberation Army (SPLA). After we left Pibor, the SPLA occupied our area, and in fact, made our house their headquarters.

But again, I'm getting ahead of our story.

Actually, I taught Idris from April to early July 1982, when we were scheduled to go to RVA for Cathy's high school graduation. Then we would fly to Waco, Texas, to help her get started in her nursing course at Baylor University. All during our many surgical procedures at Pibor, I had tried to prepare her to understand that working in a US hospital was going to be much different – especially in the realm of sterile techniques. She was undaunted and still wanted her nursing career. In fact, she finished high in her class and has become a very good nurse – despite her early training at Pibor. In 2004, she got her master's degree in nursing, and evidently has become very proficient, especially with her sterile techniques.

Back to Idris. He and Alawia were married six years. She birthed two children, Sarah and Benjamin. After Benjamin's birth, she became very depressed. The next thing she did was unbelievable to us, but she poured kerosene on her clothes and lit a match. She was severely burned. We sent her by plane to Kenya, trying to save her life, but she died.

Later, Idris married Mary, and they had four children to add to Sarah and Benjamin. Their names are Paul, Hannah, Joshua and Rachel. They continued living in Juba. One day, something awful happened. Someone threw a hand grenade into their yard, around 7:30 in the morning. That was in 1993, when hundreds of displaced people from the suburbs of Juba were running for fear of their lives. They had taken refuge in Idris and Mary's compound, but everyone was in the back yard at that time. No one was hurt because the grenade was thrown into the front yard of their house. God's blessing.

Idris was arrested several times and tortured in 1995 and 1997, when Southern Sudan was under an Islamic regime. He was arrested again in 2013, this time under a Communist regime, ruled by the Dinka tribe.

After one of the first arrests he was flown to Khartoum and then on to Kenya for treatment. When he arrived back in Khartoum, on his return trip to Juba, he heard that Sarah, his firstborn, was in Khartoum with a very serious ear infection. He delayed his trip back to Juba to find her and take care of her. She never regained her hearing. While in Khartoum, he was asked to pastor a Murle Church, which he felt called to accept, but he needed to return to Juba for the rest of his family. After bringing them back with him, he pastored this Murle church in Khartoum for ten years. While in Juba collecting his family to move to Khartoum, he didn't get to return to Pibor to visit his extended family, who lived near there.

We never heard why he was arrested again and tortured. This last time he had many bruises and a broken jaw. It was a miracle he was released at all. He was again allowed to go to Khartoum for medical treatment. Each time after an investigation of the charges made against him, he was cleared and released. At the time of this writing, he was living in Juba, pastoring a small church that met in his home. I'm sure he would appreciate your prayers, as would all the Murle.

CHAPTER 14

Leaving And A New Direction

Ginny's speaking.

SAYING GOOD-BYE AGAIN

This time we were saying good-bye to our Murle friends. Our last Sunday at church was very sad for me, Ginny. I had taught these women for a long time, and soon I wouldn't see them for a long time. As I told them good-bye, I was crying, and I guess they had never seen me cry. Early the next morning, as we were leaving, I looked out and saw several of them standing there. Usually when they visited me at our house, I always drank tea with them, but all my dishes were packed now. I went outside to explain to them why I couldn't fix tea this morning. They quickly told me they didn't want any tea. They had come to tell me they knew they were in a covenant relationship with God and they were not going back on Satan's road after I left. They thought I was crying because I thought they would return to their old lifestyle. My tears had worried them and they had come to assure me they would follow Jesus with no turning back. What a blessing their visit was to my heart. **Eternal Fruit.**

Sam's speaking.

A NEW DIRECTION IN LIFE

Jon Arensen had mentioned to us before we left Pibor that he would like us to help him with the Murle New Testament translation, but we had dismissed the idea, thinking he was just being nice because he knew we had become interested in Bible translation. True, we had learned quite a bit of the Murle language, but by no figment of anyone's imagination were we the linguistic experts we assumed all Bible translators must be.

However, during our year in the US, Jon called us from New York (we were in Texas) to ask us again if we could help with the Murle New Testament translation. He assured us we didn't have to be expert linguists, but we did have to enroll in the Wycliffe Summer Institute of Linguistics course to be held at the University of Oklahoma in June. This became our primary prayer request for the next few days. As we prayed about it, we began to feel the Lord truly was leading in that direction.

We wondered if our Southern Baptist Mission Board would approve of this development. We are always slow learners concerning God's ways. If the Lord truly was leading in that direction, then He surely would have prepared our mission board – and we found He had. They gave us their full support and paid our expenses at the University of Oklahoma. So, we signed up for the linguistic and Bible translation courses we needed. These courses were way over our heads, but in the Lord's own miraculous way, He provided us with enough wisdom to learn all we needed to join the translation team, even making passing grades.

JUBA ON THE NILE

In September of 1983, we found ourselves back in Juba, living at the Wycliffe compound on the Nile, fully engaged in the Murle New Testament translation project. We sadly learned the rebel forces had occupied Pibor and it would be impossible for us to return there. Now we had to get used to living and running a household in Juba, and naturally nobody in Juba knew Murle. That was the only Sudanese language we knew. Most people in Juba, especially in the market, spoke a language known as Juba Arabic. Therefore, one of us had to study that language while we also worked every day in Murle with our translators. That lot fell to me, since Ginny said she was convinced she would lose all her Murle if she tried to learn Arabic at the same time.

So, I had to go to the market and the other small shops two or three times a week and shop for most of our food and supplies. The Wycliffe missionaries did have a commissary on the compound that had some staples such as flour, sugar, powdered milk, etc., but all the fresh vegetables and meat and chickens and other perishables had to be bought in the market and small shops in town. Our translation team usually ate the noon meal with us, so we had to buy enough for us, plus them every week.

We ate lots of beans and lentils during those days, and always had some yogurt aging in our kitchen because the Murle guys really liked the sour yogurt with their beans, lentils and rice. That was easily doable since we had a good supply of powdered milk. One of the most plentiful vegetables in the Juba market was eggplant. We had eaten enough of that when we first got to Juba and didn't ever want any more of that.

We enjoyed the translation work very much and the Lord used it to teach us many things about the scriptures that we had not learned up to that time. We were working with a team of Murle translators. One was John Atiel, who had helped Jon in his translation work at Pibor. Another was Orozu, a teacher whom the Lord had impressed to join us. The third was John Kajac, the high school student who fell out of the tree trying to get the honey. He knew very little English, which proved to be very good. By mainly knowing Murle, he could help keep the Murle translation from being overly influenced by the English structure. Every language has its own rhythm and way of flowing. If the Murle New Testament translation was patterned after the English structure, it would never read right.

By the time we joined them, Jon had translated nine books of the New Testament. We spent six to eight hours a day translating and revising. Since we knew about what our translators could understand with their limited English vocabulary, we would first do a "front translation." That meant we put the scriptures into a simple form of English. Then they would translate this into Murle and then we would get them to read it back to us in Murle and explain what they had read. This way we had sort of a double check on the progress of our translation.

WE MOVE AGAIN

However, we were only able to stay in Juba until March of 1984, when the civil war heated up even more and moved closer to Juba. Our Murle guys began to get nervous, saying that if fighting came to Juba, they would be in great danger since they were so far away from their homes. They said if fighting came to Juba, they wanted to be in Pibor.

Without much hope of success, we applied for passports and travel documents for our three Murle team members, with the intent of moving the whole project to Kenya. To our surprise, the government issued all that was needed for us to move them. So, the translation project moved to Kenya. When we arrived in Kenya, it became evident to us why we, as Southern Baptists, were actually on this team. It is so good to know our Lord is in control of all circumstance and provides abundantly for His children and for His work. And He does this before we know we even need it.

Our mission had a large retreat center near Limuru, Kenya, called Brackenhurst Baptist Conference Center. Because we were still a part of this mission too, we were able to get places for the whole Murle team to live, plus rooms for the translation offices. Since I was a doctor, and they needed a doctor at a clinic in Nairobi, Ginny and I were given a house and a mission vehicle to help with our transportation while in Kenya. So, one day every week I went to Nairobi and supervised the Muthare Valley clinic in one of the main slum areas of the city.

Jon and Barbara remained in Sudan during those days because he was the senior missionary with Wycliffe at that time. He was needed to supervise the Wycliffe ministry there until the Sudan supervisor returned to the field to relieve him of that duty. So, for about six months we were alone with our Murle translation team until the Arensens were able to join us in Kenya. At that time, Jon would assume his rightful place and finish the project. They joined us in the fall of 1984.

Since we were no longer needed with the translation team, our mission asked us to travel to Zimbabwe for six months, where I would supervise the Gokwe clinics I had started back in 1964. Another doctor would come in May to relieve me.

As I said before, Jon had finished nine books of the New Testament when we started with the project. By the time we left the project in December 1984, after working together with Jon and the translators, twenty-five books had been completed. That left only two more books for Jon and the team to complete. According to Wycliffe scholars, the two most difficult books of the New Testament to translate are 1 and 2 Corinthians. Those were the two that remained.

Of course, after the first translated draft of any book of the Bible, many revisions need to be made. However, for us this was simplified by the acquisition of computers. We bought our first computer in 1984. Then we taught the Murle translators to type so they could type each evening whatever changes we had made during the day.

Before we got the computer, Ginny spent many hours typing the original and then retyping the changes. Then as even more changes were made, she had to type a new copy each time. Many days she typed late into the night. But that was in the days when we only had a typewriter. The use of computers has simplified Bible translation work a hundred-fold, and it has saved tons of paper and hundreds of man hours typing and editing. We started our translation work in the ancient era before computers and finished it in the modern-day computer age.

CHAPTER 15

Our Last Thoughts

LAST THOUGHTS

We were inspired to write this book because of all the wonderful things that have happened in Murle-land since we left there in 1982. These developments proved to us that discipleship is truly God's plan to impact our world with the gospel. We have never been able to return to Pibor since we left, but we have learned many interesting things about what the Lord has done in and through the Murle people in the intervening years. These things have amazed us.

Idris remained at Pibor for almost two years after we left and he continued to make disciples, strengthening the ones who became believers. After Ginny's disciples had matured spiritually, she had spent her last months at Pibor trying to teach Mama and John Kajac some English, hoping they might someday be able to help in a Murle Old Testament translation. She really didn't have much time for that project, so it wasn't very successful. They didn't learn much English.

PETER MAMA

As you may remember, Peter Mama (changed his name from Mama to Peter Mama) was paralyzed from the waist down and could not walk. He was the boy who wanted to learn to read while Ginny was teaching the others, and when she finally stopped by his house, she discovered people from her class had been teaching him and he was caught up. So, she let her class out early and taught him on her way home each day.

Ginny teaching literacy in her Murle classroom We had prayed for a miracle, hoping he might walk again, but God had other plans for him. In fact, he became a great literacy teacher and evangelist in spite of the fact that he could not walk. Because he couldn't walk, all the people knew exactly where to find him. They would come to his house and then carry him to their village. He would stay there until a good number could read and understand the gospel and be able to teach others to read. In other words, he was making disciples who, in turn, could make other disciples. Then the people of another village would come to find him and carry him to their village, and the process would begin again. So, he became an itinerant teacher-witness whom the Lord has used in a mighty way. **Eternal Fruit.**

DISCIPLESHIP SPREADING

Another way discipleship spread was when Ginny's disciples took her literacy and Bible teachings to the cattle camps every year. In that way, many people from other parts of the tribe were evangelized and taught to read. Also, after Idris left Pibor to go back to Bible school, all his disciples continued their witness and the Lord blessed all these contacts very much. **Eternal Fruit!** During the ensuing years, Idris has been able to make several trips to Pibor to strengthen the disciples and encourage them in their ministry in Murle-land. He reported to us in 2003 that despite all the trials since 1982, there were fifty-one churches in the Murle area.

However, other tribes of Southern Sudan had always had an animosity toward the Murle because of past tribal wars and because the Murle had stubbornly maintained good relations with the hated northern government. Because the Murle tribe was numerically much smaller than the Dinka, Nuer, and Shilluk tribes the surrounded them, the Murle actually looked to the northern government for protection when the other tribes tried to take their land and cattle.

So, once John Garang, a Dinka who was the leader of the mostly Dinka SPLA (Rebel forces) moved his headquarters to our empty house at Pibor, in only a short time there were differences and antagonism between his forces and the Murle. I don't recall how long he was able to stay there, but fighting erupted several times, and at one time we even heard his forces had killed Peter Mama. We were very sad at that news.

Then in the late nineties, we heard Peter Mama was not dead but alive. We heard he was in a refugee camp in Uganda, attending high school. Today, in 2020, Peter Mama is living in Juba, taking care of his family. He married and has children. One of his children was bed-ridden after a severe illness. Pray for him and his family as they care for this child.

We also heard (we have no proof) the Murle tribe became the evangelical tribe of Southern Sudan. It is a pretty big statement, but we know it could certainly be true. We and our prayer partners have been praying God would use the Murle to evangelize many people in the other surrounding tribes. We believe He has. **Eternal Fruit!**

RETURN TO KENYA

We were able to return to Kenya as volunteers in 1999, staying until June 2001. In April 2000, we were able to connect with Sudanese friends again when we spent four months ministering at a refugee camp in northern Kenya, called Kakuma Refugee Camp. This large camp, numbering 80,000 people, was supported by the U.N. There were many Sudanese refugees there. It was wonderful to see some of our friends from Pibor and to hear firsthand what the Lord had been doing in their lives during the almost twenty years since we had left Pibor. Those who were only children when we left were now grown, married, and had children of their own living right there in that refugee camp.

THE LOST BOYS

Some of you may have seen some of the documentaries on US national television about the "Lost Boys of Sudan."

Some of those lost boys were Murle. In 1987, they started walking, first in little bands and then joining with many others to become a marching army of mostly children. They had no supplies of food or water. They were marching just to get away from the fighting in their countries, where most of their families had either been killed or taken into slavery. Along the way, many of them died of exposure, disease, starvation, and many times wild animals. But those who survived stuck together and walked thousands of miles. Eventually, they crossed crocodile-infested rivers into Ethiopia, where they stayed and were provided for until 1991, when Ethiopia fell and the new government drove the boys out. So back they went across the crocodile-infested river, where many more died from drowning or crocodiles. To the west the fighting continued, so undaunted they turned toward Kenya. Many others died in those last several hundred miles, but they continued to walk because they had heard there was a place in Kenya where the boys could stay in peace. They had heard that the UN would even supply food for hungry boys. Probably in their fatigue and discouragement and past experiences of being deprived of family and home by cruel and greedy strangers, it was hard to believe such a place could exist in this world. But it did, and this rag-tag army began walking into Kakuma Refugee Camp in the early 1990s.

By the time we arrived at Kakuma in the year 2000, the survivors of this group of boys from Sudan were well-adapted to refugee camp life. At the same time, the US government devised a plan to transport most of those "Lost Boys" to the US and give them an opportunity to find jobs and a new life here in America. Most of them have done very well and some of them have gone on to universities, and their plan, we hope, is to return to Sudan someday and help the many deprived people there.

JOHN KAJAC

John Kajac has entered the picture again. We don't know where he spent the years after the Murle New Testament was completed, but recently I (Ginny) found him in Juba again and you won't believe what he is doing. He is on the translation team with Gabriel Nyamakori (his mom was in my literacy class at Pibor while he played outside as a small boy) translating the Murle Old Testament. My dream of teaching John and Mama English so they could one day translate the Old Testament into Murle has halfway come to pass. John is doing that today in 2020.

Ginny's English class with John Kajac and Peter Mama in her "English Classroom"

PEACE IN SUDAN?

We have prayed for peace in Sudan for years and heard last year (2019) a peace treaty had been signed. Now we are praying it will hold and peace will truly come to the country of Southern Sudan. We know the gospel has thrived among the Murle. We believe it is due to the many disciples who were made, way back in 1982 when we taught the Murle about their covenant relationship with God. It changed their lives when they understood they were in a covenant relationship with God, and covenants are not broken. They passed on their covenant faith to others, who in turn kept passing it on. As we look back on Pibor Post and the Murle, we can answer God's question from the first sentence of this book.

Yes, God, We Are Sure We Left Eternal Fruit In Sudan.

Epilogue

Ginny's speaking.

My friend Mollie insisted that I must tell you some more of our stories from Africa. I will begin with Mr. Wong.

MR. WONG

When we arrived in one of the countries where we served, the Peace Corp was pulling out all its personnel. One of the girls was teaching English at the Chinese Consulate. I have taught English in lots of places, so I asked her if I could take over her class when she left. She agreed if her class agreed to accept me. On her last day of class, she asked me to go with her so she could introduce me. She explained to them who I was and told them I could continue to teach the class if they agreed for me to be their teacher. They did agree, so the following week I began teaching English to a small group there in the Chinese Consulate.

After a few months, Sam and I took a short vacation to the USA to see our children and families. While there, a friend who also taught an English class of Chinese brought me some English/Chinese New Testaments she used in her class. She suggested I might use them in my class when we returned. I could have reminded her that this was a Communist consulate, but I didn't. I took the New Testaments back with me and put them on a high self in our office. I never expected to use them.

One day during my quiet time (devotional), I felt God whisper to my heart, "Take the New Testaments to class today." I argued with God because I did not want to do it. I reminded Him this was a Communist consulate. When the time came to go to class, I knew I had to be obedient, so I put one in the bottom of the bag I always took with me. I was sure I wouldn't need it.

I had noticed the people in the consulate never left anyone alone in the room with another person. They were always spying on each other. But suddenly I found myself alone in the room with Mr. Wong. God said to my heart, "Now." I was terrified, but put my hand down into my bag and dug out the New Testament. I told him I had found this book while I was in America and because it was written half in English and half in Chinese on each page, I wanted to suggest we study it in our class. I added I felt sure it would help their English.

Mr. Wong was a very somber man, and as he looked at me he asked, "And what is the name of this book?"

Hesitantly I replied, "It is called The Bible."

He stepped toward me and jerked it out of my hand and said, "My grandmother was a Christian and I have been searching for this book all of my life. Yes, we will study this book."

I could not believe my ears. The thought ran through my mind: *What if I hadn't obeyed God today? I would have missed one of the greatest blessings of my life.*

My question to you is this: Have you ever failed to obey God when He spoke to your heart to do something or go somewhere? Maybe you missed out on a wonderful blessing from God. I pray you will get that blessing next time.

FAITH/SUGAR

We listened to a lot of cassette tapes on the mission field and read lots of books because we wanted to continue to grow in our relationship with God. We were usually isolated because Sam felt he could reach more people for the Lord if he went out to where they lived. So mobile clinic work was our lifestyle for many years.

One time someone sent us a set of eighteen cassette tapes by Manley Beasley on faith. I was sure no one could preach eighteen times on one subject and I was determined to listen to all of them. This is how he defined faith: Faith is acting as if something is so, when it is not so, in order for it to be so." Then he would add, "When you know you have had a word from the Lord, then you begin to thank God for that thing." But there is one more thing you must do. You must ask someone to thank God with you, like getting out on a limb with you for that thing.

The previous time when we had been in Addis for some reason, we had heard about a lady who had some boxer puppies. We had asked her for one, but she said they were all promised. We had wanted a puppy for Cathy because her brothers were in boarding school in Addis and she was lonely. She was in the third grade and I was her teacher. As I began to ask God for something to "faith" one day during my prayer time, a boxer dog came to mind. I believed it had come from the Lord, so I asked Cathy if she would thank God with me for a boxer puppy. Of course she would, so from that day until we went to Addis the next time, we thanked God for a boxer puppy.

The first thing Cathy wanted to do the next trip we made to Addis was to go get her dog. A friend standing nearby heard her tell me to hurry to go get her puppy and he asked me if we were getting a puppy. I knew he wanted one too, so I said, "I think so." I had been thanking God for this puppy for several months, and here I was acting like I didn't know. I was convicted. All the way to the house of the lady with the puppies, I begged God to forgive me.

The lady was not at home, but her next door neighbor was our friend, so we went to her house. We told her about our praying and "faithing" a boxer puppy and she was excited too. When her neighbor arrived home, she stepped out on her side porch and told her neighbor about us and about our praying for one of her puppies.

The neighbor stopped what she was doing, looked over at us, because we were on the side porch too, and said, "No one has ever prayed for one of my pups. Little girl, come right over and pick one out. There are three left."

Cathy almost flew over to her house and soon returned with Sugar. Her puppy already had a name. All I could do was praise the Lord . We told how God used Sugar to help us get out of Ethiopia in **Truth On Trial,** our other book.

SCREENS FOR GSS

Our boys were at Good Shepherd School, a boarding school near Addis Ababa. It was by the city dump with millions of flies everywhere around it. The boys complained a lot about the flies crawling all over them in their classrooms.

When I began to ask God for something else I could "faith," He gave me the word "screens." I asked Him who I was supposed to get out on a limb with and I felt it was the principal of the school. I knew him, but not well. I wasn't sure how this was going to work, but the next time we were in Addis, the day before we started back home, I drove over to his house in the late afternoon. He came out on his porch as I drove up. I jumped out of the car and shouted out to him that I needed him to thank God with me for screens for GSS. (I felt sure he would be happy to have screens.) I asked him not to spend any gift that came to the school, because I was sure God was going to send the money for screens. Then I jumped back in the car and left.

I thanked the Lord every day for this money, but several months passed and none came in. I knew if I asked my brother in the States, he would send me the money, but I also knew that would be cheating. I was thanking **God** for sending the money.

During this time, I received a letter from an older couple in my home church in Hollandale, Mississippi. They said they were coming to Addis and hoped to see me. No one from my town had ever come to Africa, much less Addis, and I was determined to go to town while they were there to see them. We had a wonderful visit.

When they were leaving, the husband looked at me and said, "Ginny, what are you praying for?"

I had never imagined they would be the answer to my prayer of thanksgiving. I told him about the screens, and he took out his checkbook and wrote me a rather large check, enough for the screens.

Our next furlough I was speaking at my church and this couple was there. I told this story, and when I finished, he stood up right there in church and said, "I need to tell the end of this story." He said when he took out his checkbook to write the check, he had no intention of giving me as much money as he did. But it was like someone was holding his hand as he wrote down the amount, and he was amazed at how much he had given me. Thank You, Lord.

STAN

You have read about our two boys in this book, but I wanted to tell you more about Stan. After finishing college, he went to Baylor University to get a master's degree in geology. He chose to study about water instead of oil. While there, he spent a lot of time helping international students who were having a hard time adjusting. As parents, we wondered if he would ever finish and kept pushing him. He had found the love of his life too. They were engaged, but put off the wedding for a year. He wanted to return to Ethiopia as a volunteer in water development after the bad famine during that year.

On March 18, 1989, while on a trip to Addis with one of his Ethiopian friends, Stan pulled off the road by a deep gorge to take pictures. When he backed up to get on the road, his back tire went over the cliff. His friend at first told us Stan pushed him out, but later said he jumped out. It doesn't matter. The truck rolled down the cliff, but Stan was thrown out and died instantly. He joined the Lord that day. Someone found his tape recorder and we found what they had been listening to. The tape was by Sandi Patty and the tape was still on the song, "We Shall Behold Him." It was sooner than he thought.

We were on the Island of Zanzibar when the news came. Sam had gone fishing that day so Alex, our guard, and I sat on the front steps and cried until Sam arrived. We flew to Ethiopia and had Stan's funeral there in Ethiopia as soon as Elizabeth, his fiancée arrived with her dad. Patents don't expect to bury their children, but sometimes we have to. I know I will see him one day because he is waiting for me in heaven. Elizabeth got the wedding invitations the day Stan died. Her story has a happy ending: she is happily married now with three lovely children.

THE COPY MACHINE

On the island of Zanzibar, while Sam was working in the V.I. Linin hospital, I was teaching English to students who had graduated from the twelfth grade but needed to learn more English before they applied to college. There were no books, so I had to write my own lessons. I used our copy machine a lot.

We didn't have many visitors, but one day we heard a lady was coming to stay with us for several days. It was hot on Zanzibar. We knew she would need a fan in her room but there was no electrical outlet. The only thing we knew to do was run an extension cord from our office over near her room so she could have a fan. That meant the copy machine was going to be on the same extension cord. It was fine all the time of her visit. After she left, instead of plugging the copy machine back into the main outlet in the office, I just left it as it was. It had been working.

Sam ran in one day and wanted a copy of a letter, so I went back to make a copy for him, but when I turned it on, I heard a terrible noise and the letters EO flashed at me.

I grabbed the manual that came with it and found EO. It said the machine was broken and needed to be taken to the nearest dealer. Being on an island meant we would have to fly it to Tanzania or Kenya. I felt sick.

We were having a Bible study that night in our house and one of the men said, "Ginny, you pray for people to be healed, so why not pray for the copy machine to be healed?"

I explained to him that I was the reason it was broken because I had been too lazy to change the plug into the right outlet. I couldn't ask God to heal my mistake.

The next morning during my quiet time, I was reading in **John 15:7,** which says: **If you remain in me and my words remain in you, ask whatever you wish and it will be done for you.**" I felt God telling me we could pray for the copy machine. I ran back to the office where Sam was having his devotions and burst in to tell him we could pray for the copy machine. We stood beside it, put our hands on it and thanked God for healing it. I turned it on and it was perfect. What a blessing to have it working again. There was a lot of praising God in our house that day. When we left Zanzibar, I wanted to take that copy machine with me because it felt almost like family, but it belonged to the mission.

SAM

Perhaps you noticed I didn't include Sam when I said I knew I would see Stan in heaven one day. I should have included Sam, because he died in 2017. He left me to finish this book, which has taken me a long time. I want to share one other thing about him with you.

He had already finished medical school when we married, but he always wanted me to see his medical school: The

University of Texas Medical School in Galveston. We had our first wedding anniversary in Africa, so we didn't have time to visit Galveston before we left for the mission field. When we did get there, he took me right to the cadaver lab. I decided this must have been a special place for him. Long before he died, he told me he wanted to give his body to a medical school to be used as a cadaver. We filled out papers and he signed them.

In 2019, two years after Sam's death, the University of Oklahoma Medical School sent me a letter saying they were going to use Sam's body as a cadaver the next school year. The letter went on to say they had a program where the immediate family of that person was invited to come to the medical school on a chosen day to talk to the med students who would be using that body for study. They wanted the med students to know the cadaver had been a real person and they needed to treat it with respect.

Cathy and two grandsons went with me to the school that day. I was able to talk about Sam and his life as a missionary with the students for an hour. What a joy that was for me. The students were very attentive and thanked me for sharing. I also took four of our books, **Truth On Trial,** to give them. But that isn't all. The school invited me back to visit with the students when they finished their class.

They asked me to bring a framed picture of Sam. When Cathy and I got there, we saw a table with all the names of the people used as cadavers spaced around it. (Sam wasn't the only cadaver, of course.) I put his picture by his name. Also, beside each name and picture was a vase with a white rose in it. During the program, one student from each group was asked to come and stand by the name of their cadaver. Then when that name was called, that student picked up the rose and brought it to us. It was a lovely ending to their program.

Actually, that wasn't all. When we opened the door to leave, there was a table full of refreshments and our group of med students standing there to greet and visit with us. They told us about their class. I had only taken four of our **Truth On Trial** books when I went the first time because I thought there would only be four students; there were eight. This time I took four more with me. When I asked if they wanted them, the other four grabbed them from my hands. Now I am praying they will read it. It was wonderful to know that Sam had one last time to give his testimony to a group of med students and to know that his testimony would live on even further in our book.

I believe these are enough stories for today. I pray that God will bless you, that you will have a desire to find disciples so you can teach them what it means to be in a covenant relationship with God, and that you will be filled with joy because of your **Eternal Fruit.**

Ginny and Sam. We hope you have enjoyed our time with you.

CPSIA information can be obtained
at www.ICGtesting.com
Printed in the USA
LVHW012138060221
678613LV00048B/1155